Build Your Own PC Home Entertainment System

Brian Underdahl

McGraw-Hill/Osborne

New York   Chicago   San Francisco   Lisbon   London   Madrid   Mexico City
Milan   New Delhi   San Juan   Seoul   Singapore   Sydney   Toronto

The McGraw·Hill Companies

McGraw-Hill/Osborne
2600 Tenth Street
Berkeley, California 94710
U.S.A.

To arrange bulk purchase discounts for sales promotions, premiums, or fund-raisers, please contact **McGraw-Hill/Osborne** at the above address. For information on translations or book distributors outside the U.S.A., please see the International Contact Information page immediately following the index of this book.

Build Your Own PC Home Entertainment System

234567890 QPD QPD 019876543

ISBN 0-07-222769-9

Publisher
Brandon A. Nordin

Vice President & Associate Publisher
Scott Rogers

Acquisitions Editor
Franny Kelly

Project Editor
Janet Walden

Acquisitions Coordinator
Martin Przybyla

Technical Editor
Jim Kelly

Copy Editor
William McManus

Proofreader
Pam Vevea

Indexer
Claire Splan

Series Design
Jean Butterfield

Illustrators
Melinda Moore Lytle
Michael Mueller
Lyssa Wald

Cover Series Design
Ted Holladay

Cover Illustration
Ted Holladay

This book was composed with Corel VENTURA™ Publisher.

*This book is dedicated to all of the great pioneers
who kept on tinkering and thus made it
possible for us to have such
awesome computing
power at our
fingertips.*

About the Author

Brian Underdahl is the well-known, best-selling author of over 65 computer books covering a broad range of topics. He has appeared on a number of television shows, including *The Computer Chronicles* and several *TechTV* programs. His books have won awards, including an Award of Merit from the Northern California Technical Communications Competition.

Brian understands that computers can be confusing—especially when all the high-tech gurus seem to want to use jargon to confuse ordinary people rather than plain English to help enlighten them. That's why Brian's books are different; he takes the time to explain what's going on so that you can understand the subjects easily. He figures that it's the author who should do the work so that you, dear reader, can get your money's worth.

Contents at a Glance

Contents

Acknowledgments

An author is a very lucky person because it's their name that goes on the cover of their books. It would be very unfair, however, to think that the author created the book all alone. That's why I feel it's so important to acknowledge and thank the many people who have made such important contributions to this project. They include **Franny Kelly**, **Janet Walden**, **Scott Rogers**, **Brandon A. Nordin**, **Martin Przybyla**, and all of the other great people at McGraw-Hill/Osborne Media Group for making this book possible, and for all their great help along the way.

Thanks also to:

❏ **Jim Kelly** for his excellent technical review.

❏ **Antec** for the case we used to hold the project.

❏ **MSI** for the terrific motherboard.

❏ **AMD** for supplying the Athlon XP processor.

❏ **Crucial Technology** for the top-quality memory.

❏ **ATI** for the top-notch video board.

❏ **Planar** for the gorgeous LCD monitor.

❏ **Logitech** for the cordless keyboard, mouse, and trackball.

❏ **Maxtor** for the perfect hard drive choice.

❏ **Altec Lansing** for the awesome speaker system.

❏ **Pinnacle** for a selection of excellent products, including both hardware and software.

❏ **Terk** for the video distribution system and the amplified antenna.

❏ **SnapStream** for the SnapStream PVS software.

❏ **Trip Thomas** for his excellent assistance.

❏ **Andy Marken** and **Linda Herd** for providing a number of important items.

I know I've forgotten to include mention of some people who really belong here. If you're one of them, I apologize for this gaffe.

Introduction

In this book I'm going to show you how to have some fun, save some money, and end up with a killer home entertainment system that will simply blow away anything you can buy off the shelf. You're going to see how you can easily create a customized PC-based system that will deliver all of the multimedia action you could want without being some monstrosity that fills your living room with all sorts of wires, cables, and other ugly junk. In other words, not only is this going to deliver the entertainment you want, but it's also going to look good enough so that not even the pickiest spouse (or significant other) is going to have a reason to complain.

Over the years since PCs were first introduced, a lot of people have had fun pushing the limits; they've customized their factory-built PCs, upgraded components, and in some cases have built an entire system from readily available parts. A lot of what they did almost bordered on a black art, and little of it resulted in something you'd ever want to put out on display. Well, it's time for a change—and one for the better.

Building your own home entertainment system using a PC as your starting point is going to be a very satisfying experience. I'm going to show you everything you need to know so that not only will you have fun, you'll also learn a bit, buy the best components for your needs, and still save some money. When you're done, you'll enjoy adjusting your TV watching to fit *your* schedule, listening to hours of your favorite music, watching DVD movies, and maybe even get in some time playing video games.

Before we begin, I just want to point out that you don't have to be some computer geek or expert to do all of this, either. I'm going to tell you exactly what you need to know and I'm going to include lots of photos to show you exactly what you need to do.

This book covers two different approaches to building your home entertainment system so that you can choose the method that best suits your personal needs. The main focus is to show you how to start from scratch and build the most awesome, compact home entertainment system PC you could possibly imagine. But I'm also going to show you how to save a bit by upgrading a PC you already have; after all, not everyone has the budget for an all-out new system. Either way, you'll certainly end up with a system that will provide hours of enjoyment and one you can truly say that you built yourself.

Part I

Assembling Your PC Home Entertainment System

Chapter 1
The Advantages of Building

In these days when you can buy just about anything you want off the shelf at your local megastore, building your own PC-based home entertainment system might seem like a waste of time. After all, can't you just go in, plunk down your credit card, and walk out with the *perfect* system without any extra effort on your part? The truth is, no, you probably can't. In this chapter, you'll see that you end up with a whole lot more capabilities by building it yourself, and you'll realize your efforts will be worthwhile.

If you're still asking yourself whether building your own PC—no matter what its purpose—is something you really can do, don't worry. As you'll see soon enough, you don't have to be a technical wizard; you just have to follow some simple directions. And as you'll see in this brief chapter, assembling your own home entertainment system PC will bring you a lot of enjoyment for years to come.

Get Just What You Want

One of the biggest problems with buying a PC off the shelf for your home entertainment system hub is simply that you aren't going to get what you *really* want. Oh sure, it may have some of the components that sound like what you want, like a TV tuner card, a DVD-ROM drive, and so on, but it's pretty unlikely that those components will really be the *best* ones. To make matters worse, you may not even be able to get an accurate list of just what is in the box. Just try asking the sales clerk to tell you the exact brand and model of the video card or the hard drive, for example. You've got a better chance of getting an accurate answer regarding the winning numbers in the next lottery drawing. And forget about asking the store to swap out the components you want to upgrade—unless you want to pay a whole lot extra, that is.

Assembling your home entertainment system PC yourself is the best way to get *just what you want*. When you're making the decisions, you can be sure you're getting the right pieces to build a home entertainment system hub that delivers the excitement and entertainment to your living room that you expect. Forget all the compromises; this is one system that will serve up the kinds of entertainment options you really want.

By the way, you may have heard about the new Windows XP Media Center Edition PCs and wondered if they might be a reasonable alternative to building your own PC-based home entertainment system hub. The short answer is no. The slightly longer answer is that although the manufacturers of the Windows XP Media Center Edition PCs are adding some types of features similar to those we'll be including, their systems have some serious compromises that limit their usefulness. For example, with our system, you'll be able to record whatever you want, unlike with the Windows XP Media Center Edition PCs, which limit what you can record. With a Windows XP Media Center Edition PC, you can't record a show and then play it back anywhere else. With the home entertainment system PC, you can play your recordings anywhere.

Let's take a quick look at some of the advanced features you can have by building your own home entertainment system PC. This isn't a complete list, of course, but it will give you some ideas about just how fun this is going to be. While you're looking through this list, remember that this system will also end up being an extremely capable general-purpose PC, too, so you'll also be able to do things like balance your checkbook and surf the Web—all from the comfort of your living room sofa.

Personal Video Recorder

Have you ever been watching your favorite TV show and had the phone ring just when something really important was coming on? Have you ever noticed how many commercials the networks seem to slip into an hour of programming? Have you ever been watching a TV show and saw something so incredible that you wished you could get an instant replay? If any of these scenarios sound familiar, you're probably a good candidate for a *personal video recorder (PVR)*.

Just what is a personal video recorder? A PVR is a PC that saves your TV shows as data on a hard drive. This enables you to pause live TV, instantly skip forward past the commercials, watch one show while another is being recorded, and even save your favorite episodes onto a disc for later viewing. In other words, a PVR serves as a high-powered VCR that's been pumped up with a whole bunch of computing power.

One of the most outstanding features of our home entertainment system project will be the built-in PVR. Your TV viewing will never be the same once you've experienced ultimate control over how and when you watch your favorite shows.

By the way, you can buy a stand-alone PVR, such as TiVo or ReplayTV, but you won't be able to use it for anything except as a PVR. The TiVo and ReplayTV units simply don't offer nearly as much as you'll get from your home entertainment system PC. Sure, they'll record TV shows, but continue on through this chapter and see how much else they can't do that your custom-built PC can easily do.

Audio Jukebox

How would you like to be able to program literally hundreds of hours of music, create your own mixes, include the latest MP3s you download from the Internet, and never have to touch another audio CD? Well, that's really just the tip of the iceberg in terms of what you can do using the audio capabilities of your home entertainment system PC. Once you've built your system, you'll have total control over your music listening.

You'll want top-quality sound, so we're going to build six-speaker, Dolby 5.1 sound features into the home entertainment system. Not only that, but you'll have the options of driving a top-quality speaker system directly or of sending a clean, digital audio signal to a high-end component amplifier via your choice of optical or coax cables. Figure 1-1 shows an example of a great speaker system you can connect directly to the home entertainment system.

Figure 1-1
This Altec Lansing 5100 speaker system is a great addition to the home entertainment system.

In addition to playing MP3s downloaded from the Internet, you'll also be able to play audio CDs as well as create your own MP3 or WMA files from your audio CDs. That way, you'll really have control over your musical selections since you'll be able to play just the songs you like and skip the ones you don't like. You can even set up different play lists for different occasions.

DVD Player and Recorder

You expect a home entertainment system to be able to play recorded movies, and the one in our project handles that task quite nicely with the ability to play DVDs. What you might not expect is the ability to record your own DVDs so that you can archive your favorite shows, too. Well, you may not have expected it, but with the availability of high-performance yet reasonably priced DVD-RW drives, it is a natural addition.

By adding a DVD-RW drive, you not only can save your favorite TV shows onto inexpensive discs, but also create your own DVD-based presentations using your digital camcorder as well as images from your digital camera. And since DVD-RW drives can also record onto inexpensive CD-R and CD-RW discs, you can easily create audio CDs that contain your favorite music for use in the CD player in your car, too.

Custom Appearance

Another big advantage of building your own PC-based home entertainment system is that you can build a system that actually looks good enough to fit into your living room. Somehow the basic beige of a standard PC just isn't going to cut it, is it? Well, when you're building your own PC, you have a whole lot more flexibility in designing something you'll be proud to have others see.

There are any number of excellent appearance options you may want to consider. Something like a custom color for the computer's case is a good place to start. For example, the Antec Plus660AMG case, shown in Figure 1-2, comes in a stunning metallic silver gray. Actually, though, when you're building the unit from scratch, you do have the option of painting it any color you like to match your own décor (you can even paint the Antec case if you want something other than metallic silver gray).

Figure 1-2
You'll want a good-looking case like this one for your home entertainment system PC.

I'll discuss more important details about choosing the proper case in Chapter 2.

Ultimate Game System

While you're building your home entertainment system PC, why not add in the right components necessary to make it into the ultimate PC gaming system? After all, computer games do provide a lot of entertainment value, and you really won't have to add very many components to be able to play some games. Something like Logitech's WingMan Extreme Digital 3D joystick shown in Figure 1-3 may actually be just about all you need if the rest of the system is configured properly.

Figure 1-3
A few simple pieces can make your home entertainment system PC into a gaming system.

As you'll see in later chapters, we'll be choosing system components that can easily keep up with the demands of most computer games. Here, too, a little advance planning will certainly pay off.

Internet Radio

I could go on, but for now I'll just mention one more way you can use your new home entertainment system PC to provide some additional entertainment value that no ordinary home entertainment center can match. If you have access to a broadband Internet connection, why not use your global options and listen to radio stations from around the world? You'll instantly have your choice of thousands of different stations carrying every imaginable type of programming. Even if you live in one of the largest metropolitan centers on Earth, your over-the-air choices will be no match for your Internet radio choices. And the best part is that this feature won't cost you anything extra.

You'll soon see that building your own home entertainment system PC opens up a whole world of new entertainment options. Ordinary home entertainment equipment just can't stack up!

Saving Money

If all of these capabilities sound like they're going to cost a ton of money, you're in for a very pleasant surprise. Even if you follow my recommendations and buy the top-quality components I'll show you for your system, the total price will be far less than what you would pay for an equivalent system from one of the PC manufacturers.

I'd like to make an important point about buying the components to build your home entertainment system PC. You'll notice that I'm not going to be quoting very many specific prices. To be honest, those prices change so fast that any numbers I might mention wouldn't do you much good anyway. Likewise, I'm not going to discuss specific places to buy the various bits and pieces you'll need. In the end, you'll have a list of recommended components, and that's when you can start shopping.

What is important is that you shop around to get the best deal. Be sure to consider all of the hidden charges, too. Keep in mind that vendors who offer lowball prices may actually be more expensive if they charge outrageous shipping and handling amounts.

By the way, finding the best prices on the Web can be a real challenge. You may want to get some help from a program like Copernic Agent Professional (www.copernic.com), which can find you the best prices by looking at a whole bunch of web sites at the same time (see Figure 1-4). Copernic Agent also comes in a free, ad-supported version, but I highly recommend paying the small fee to get the Professional version since it has so many additional useful features you'll continue to use it long after you've finished this project. I talk more about this really great tool in Chapter 7.

Figure 1-4
Copernic Agent
Professional can
help you get the
best deals on all
of your components.

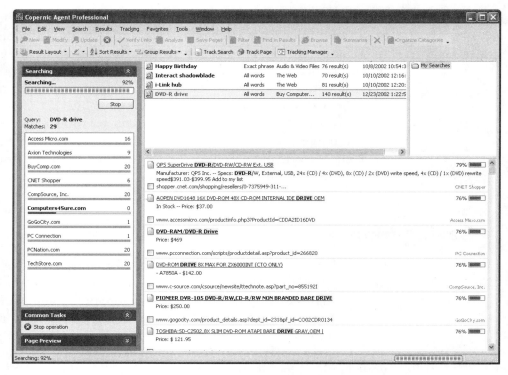

Customizing a PC You Already Own

Even though my main focus in this book is showing you how to build the ultimate home entertainment system PC from scratch, I realize that such an all-out approach simply may not be in your budget. Well, that's not a problem, because I'm also going to talk about some options for those of you who might want to upgrade a PC you already own.

In fact, a few simple upgrades can add a lot of new capabilities, so you can have a customized home entertainment system PC for a very small investment. It may not have all the bells and whistles of a system you would build from scratch, but you'll still get a lot of enjoyment out of knowing that you did it yourself!

Okay, you've seen some of the great things that a home entertainment system based on a customized PC design can do. In the next chapter, we'll get right into selecting and assembling the basic components. Get ready to have some fun.

Chapter 2
Choosing Basic Components

Tools of the Trade

To complete this chapter you'll need:

Antec Plus660AMG case
MSI KT3 Ultra2-R motherboard
AMD Athlon XP 2200+ processor
Two 512MB PC2700 DDR Crucial Technology memory modules
Windows XP
A set of screwdrivers
Nylon ties

Now we're ready to begin the process of building your PC, which will be the hub of your new home entertainment system. We'll start by looking at the basic components you need, and show you some excellent options. You can, of course, make different choices, but I strongly suggest that you read through this chapter so that you have a firm grasp of the importance of the various items before you go out and start shopping—that way you aren't nearly as likely to end up with components that don't really meet your needs.

In this chapter, we're going to consider four hardware choices as well as the operating system necessary to make the PC function. The four hardware components are closely related, and they represent the foundation upon which the entire PC will be built. The four components we'll discuss in this chapter include the case, the motherboard, the processor, and memory. As you will see, your choices in one area have a direct effect on your options in the other areas.

Choosing Your Case

In some ways, choosing a case for the home entertainment system PC should be a decision you make after you've selected a motherboard and processor. After all, the choices you make in those two components will demand certain choices in case design. On the other hand, this project is not intended as something you'll hide away under the desk in your office. This PC will be quite visible as the centerpiece of the home entertainment system in your living room, so appearance must be an important consideration.

Choosing a case involves more than simply selecting a design that you find appealing. It is also quite important to remember that the case must have adequate room for each of the components you want to add. For example, you need room for at least two drives—a hard drive and some sort of CD-ROM–compatible drive. Here are some additional things to keep in mind in selecting a case:

❑ Proper airflow is an absolute necessity since components like the system processor generate a lot of heat. Believe it or not, it is far better to have a closed case with a well-designed airflow than to leave the sides off of the case, since an open case is not as efficient at keeping the system cool.

❑ Modern computers run at frequencies that can generate a lot of electrical interference. This interference can affect radios, TVs, cordless phones, cell phones, and most any other device that depends on radio signals. Reducing the amount of radio signals that can leak out of the case is vitally important to prevent causing problems with those other devices. Once again, the design and quality of the case are major factors in insuring that such problems are kept to a minimum.

❑ Since you will be using this PC in your living room as a part of your home entertainment system, the amount of noise coming out of the PC is also very important. A PC has a number of potential noise-generating sources, but the case fans are probably the most noticeable. Keeping the sound level down depends on using high-quality, ball-bearing fans with well-designed mounting systems. Some manufacturers (such as Antec) even go a bit further by regulating fan speed so that the fans run as slowly as possible while keeping the temperature within proper operating limits.

❑ Motherboard manufacturers have agreed to certain standard form factors that specify the size of motherboards as well as the placement of various connectors (such as the keyboard and mouse ports). In choosing a case, you must select one that matches the form factor of the motherboard—otherwise the motherboard and case simply won't be compatible.

❏ Cases are available with or without a power supply. If you choose a case that does not include a power supply, you need to factor in the cost of a good-quality power supply, too.

So, with these items in mind, let's take a look at some case designs that will work for our home entertainment system PC.

Case Styles

Computer cases come in a number of different appearances, but they generally fit into certain well-defined categories. As mentioned earlier, these categories are based on the form factor of the motherboard. These days, virtually all motherboards comply with one of the ATX standards. As you will learn shortly in the section "Selecting a Motherboard," there are three common ATX designs. The primary differences between them have to do with the overall size of the circuit board and the component layouts. Since different types of motherboards have different sizes, you need to buy a case that fits the type of motherboard that you want to use.

Let's take a look at some of the common case designs.

Minitower Cases

Probably the most common type of computer case these days is what is known as a *minitower.* This is a vertical design that typically stands upright either on or under a desk. There are several reasons why the minitower case is the most popular:

❏ It is large enough to hold several different drives. This means that you are not limited to installing a single CD-ROM or DVD drive, making it easier for you to copy discs, for example.

❏ Its vertical design can be important for heat dissipation reasons. In fact, AMD specifically indicates that it does not support the use of horizontal or desktop cases with the Athlon XP processor.

❏ It often is flexible enough to be used with several different motherboard designs. This, however, is too important to assume, and you must verify the fit before you buy the case.

❏ It has enough room to accommodate several expansion boards so that you can add things like a wireless network card, a modem, a high-performance video card, and a sound card.

Other Case Designs

Minitower cases are not the only design you can use, of course. For example, here are some other case designs that I considered but then ruled out for the reasons stated:

❏ There are larger towers, sometimes referred to as *server towers*, but these really are too big for most home entertainment systems.

❏ Certain desktop cases might work, but these generally lack much expansion room. In addition, desktop cases may have heat dissipation problems that make them unsuitable for use with higher-power processors.

❏ Shuttle Computer (www.shuttleonline.com) offers a new design it calls the XPC. At first glance, the extremely compact size of the XPC, with its advanced heat pipe cooling system, looks like a perfect choice for the home entertainment system PC. Unfortunately, the XPC system has very limited expansion capabilities, and ultimately something more flexible is required to fit the goals of this project.

Another Case Design You'll Want to Avoid

Microtower *cases have all the disadvantages of desktop cases, and the ones I've seen are generally fairly poor quality, too. In fact, the owner of a shop that assembles custom-built systems told me that he simply wouldn't recommend those types of cases because they had too many compromises.*

The Project Case

Figure 2-1 shows the interior of the Antec Plus660AMG case (www.antec-inc .com) that I have selected for this project; I have removed the side panel but have not yet installed any components.

Figure 2-1
The Antec
Plus660AMG case
is well suited to
this project.

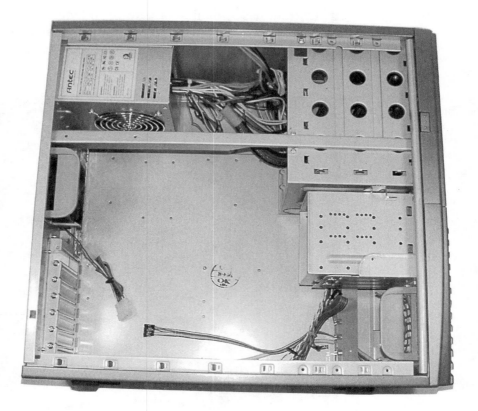

This case offers a number of important features that make it perfect for the home entertainment system PC project. In addition to having plenty of room for all the components we want to add, the Antec case offers the following advantages:

❏ Its power supply has a special connector that is used to power and control the case fans. This enables the fans to be run quite slowly under normal conditions in order to reduce fan noise. If too much heat is being generated, the fans automatically speed up to produce additional cooling. This feature makes a PC built in this case virtually silent—an important consideration for the home entertainment system PC.

❏ It includes two case fans (one of which is in the removable side panel) in addition to the two fans on the power supply. There is also a mounting bracket if you want to add yet another fan.

❏ Its front has a small door (shown in Figure 2-2) that provides two front-panel USB ports and one IEEE-1394 port. This makes it far easier for you to connect to external peripherals because you don't have to reach around behind the PC.

Figure 2-2
The Antec case offers some handy front-panel ports.

❏ It has a washable air filter, which will help keep the interior of your home entertainment system PC cleaner.

Power Supply Considerations

Even though the Antec case I've selected for this project comes with a high-quality power supply already installed, not all cases do so. But even if you do choose a case that includes a power supply, you need to make certain that the power supply can handle the demands placed on it by the components you install.

Choosing the proper power supply can seem almost like a black art. One reason for this is that it can be very difficult to determine just how much power is needed. AMD recommends sizing the power supply by adding up the power needed by all of the system components except for the processor, multiplying that value by 80 percent, and then adding the power used by the processor. Unfortunately, finding out the power drawn by each of the components is nearly impossible.

As an alternative to trying to make a precise determination of power supply draw on your own, you may simply want to use some estimates that AMD has produced. According to a white paper AMD published in May 2002, a typical PC needs a power supply of at least 165 watts, and a high-performance PC needs at least 245 watts. To be on the safe side, you'll want 300 watts. The Antec case being used for this project has a 330 watt supply.

HEADS UP!

Watch for the Correct Layout

In addition to sizing the power supply properly, you should also be aware that different power supplies can have a different layout. Most power supplies are built to conform to the ATX standard, which means they'll fit into the case properly. But just because the power supply fits doesn't mean that it has the correct configuration.

In addition to power draw considerations, a power supply needs to be constructed so that the air flows properly through the case. To see what I mean, take a look at the Antec power supply shown in Figure 2-3. The air inlet is on the bottom of the power supply rather than on the front. According to tests that engineers at AMD have performed, having the air inlet on the bottom of the power supply improves the air flow over the motherboard and the processor. The result is a system that runs cooler (and quieter if the fans can then run slower).

Figure 2-3
The location of the power supply air inlet is important.

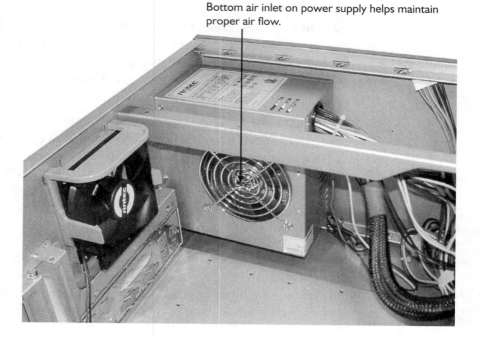

Bottom air inlet on power supply helps maintain proper air flow.

Depending on the motherboard you choose, you may need to ensure that the power supply has two extra power connectors to provide additional power to the motherboard. This type of power supply is called an ATX12V power supply, and is compatible with all ATX-type motherboards—even those that do not require the extra connectors. The Antec power supply does comply with this standard.

Selecting a Motherboard

The motherboard is, of course, one of the most important elements of your PC. It's also one of the most confusing to choose since there are so many different brands of motherboards as well as a large selection within most brands. It's frankly pretty difficult to decide on one motherboard over all of the others. Still, if you're going to assemble your own PC, you do have to pick one of them.

So how can you decide which motherboard will be the best choice for your home entertainment system PC? Here are the factors I considered:

❑ **Processor compatibility**   Each motherboard typically supports one line of processors. Those that are designed for the Intel P4 won't work with AMD Athlon XP processors (and vise versa).

❑ **Form factor**   Motherboards come in different sizes and you need one that will fit the case you've selected. We'll look at form factors in the next section.

❑ **Onboard features**   Certain motherboards include built-in capabilities that may make it unnecessary for you to buy add-ons such as sound cards, network adapters, and so on. Also, newer motherboard designs often have USB 2.0 capability, enabling you to use the much faster USB 2.0 peripherals without buying a special adapter.

❑ **Expansion capability**   All motherboards have sockets for things like the processor, memory, and expansion cards. But, depending on your needs, the expansion capabilities may be too limited to allow you to do what you want. For example, some of the smallest motherboards (in Flex-ATX format) lack an AGP slot, thus limiting you to lower-performance video.

Motherboard Form Factors

Motherboards come in several different sizes. Table 2-1 shows the maximum dimensions for each of the standard size motherboards in use today.

Name	Width (inches)	Depth (inches)
ATX	12.0	9.6
Mini-ATX (seldom used)	11.2	9.2
Micro-ATX	9.6	9.6
Flex-ATX	9.0	7.5

Table 2-1
Motherboard Dimensions

As the table shows, the standard ATX motherboard is the largest of the PC motherboards in use today. Even so, none of the standard sizes is all that large—especially when you consider all of the functionality they deliver.

No matter which size motherboard you choose, they all are supposed to conform to the ATX 2.03 standard in terms of certain layout issues. Primary among these is the positioning and configuration of the I/O panel on the back edge of the motherboard (the I/O panel is where you find the various connectors for the keyboard, the mouse, the printer, and so on). This means that the motherboard you choose is supposed to match up with the I/O shield on the back of your case without modifications. Of course, this also means that the smaller size motherboards simply have far less space for expansion card slots.

The Project Motherboard

After considering all of the factors, I selected the MSI KT3 Ultra2-R (www.msi.com) motherboard, shown in Figure 2-4. I chose the MSI KT3 Ultra2-R motherboard for a number of reasons:

Figure 2-4
The MSI KT3 Ultra2-R motherboard that is used in the home entertainment system PC

❏ It is adaptable enough to allow the use of any of several different processors (AMD Athlon XP, Athlon, and Duron), which means that you can choose the fastest processor you can afford from a number of options.

❏ It has three DDR (double data rate) memory slots that support up to 3GB of memory.

❏ It has onboard, Dolby 5.1 six-channel sound capabilities.

❏ In addition to standard ATA-133 IDE controllers, it has a Promise RAID controller (I'll discuss this more in Chapter 5), which means that you can get much faster disk performance for tasks such as video editing.

❏ It has six USB 2.0 ports (two of which we'll be able to connect to the USB ports on the front of the case).

❏ It has a AGP 4X slot for a high-performance video card, five PCI slots for expansion cards, and a CNR (communications network riser) slot for a modem or an audio card.

In addition to all of these capabilities, the MSI KT3 Ultra2-R is well respected for being very high quality. Indeed, MSI even includes the proper ATA-133 drive cables so that your high-performance disk drives can provide optimum throughput.

Processor Realities

The third item on our list of basics is the processor. Believe it or not, the home entertainment system PC demands a pretty fast processor in order to keep up with tasks such as video recording, video editing, and creating your own DVD movies. Video streams simply include so much data that any type of quality video processing requires a high-end CPU.

Intel or AMD?

There are two primary rivals in the PC processor market. Intel makes the various Pentium models and AMD makes the Athlon chips. The two companies wage a constant battle over bragging rights to the fastest CPUs—a battle in which we the consumers are the ultimate winners.

In choosing a processor for your home entertainment system PC, it's clear that either a fast Intel Pentium P4 or an AMD Athlon XP will provide the speed and application compatibility you need. In fact, you probably wouldn't notice any performance difference between a system assembled with an Intel Pentium P4 chip and a system assembled with an AMD Athlon XP chip.

You will, however, discover one huge difference when you start pricing the components for your system. An AMD Athlon XP processor typically costs about half as much as an Intel Pentium P4 with the equivalent performance. In addition, some Intel processors require much more expensive memory than the DDR memory used by the AMD CPUs.

Minimum Speeds

So just how fast a processor do you really need? That's a little hard to determine because so many different factors come into play. As a general rule, however, you'll probably want a CPU equivalent to at least 2 GHz for processing video streams.

As you can imagine, Intel and AMD disagree on processor speed ratings. In the past, Intel has always insisted on rating processors using their clock speed (although Intel has recently been discussing a new processor line that is not rated this way). AMD, on the other hand, rates its processors with a "performance equivalent" rating. The truth is probably somewhere between the two camps.

The Project Processor

To keep up with the demands of the tasks we'll ask of the home entertainment system PC while not breaking the bank by going for the fastest possible CPU, I selected the AMD Athlon XP 2200+. While the core of this processor runs at 1.8 GHz, AMD rates it as being equivalent to a P4 running at 2.2 GHz. In other words, it's exactly at our sweet spot with enough power to do the job at a reasonable price.

No matter which processor you choose, it's absolutely critical that you take the proper measures to keep it from overheating. In fact, even a few seconds of running without the correct heat sink can completely ruin the CPU. Figure 2-5 shows the TaiSol ball bearing heat sink I'm using. The processor manufacturer always lists recommended heat sinks on their web site, but the surest way to get the correct one is to buy the retail version of the processor, which includes both the CPU and the heat sink in the package.

Figure 2-5
You need a good
heat sink to protect
the processor.

Memory Minimums

Memory is sometimes treated almost as an afterthought, but it's really one of the most important factors in determining just how fast a system runs and how much it can do at one time. In fact, adding memory is often the most cost-effective performance-boosting move you can make.

We all know that there are recommended minimum levels of memory that you should have in a PC. Depending on the operating system and the types of applications you want to run, these minimum levels can vary quite a bit. Unfortunately, a lot of people make the assumption that the minimums are good enough. As a result, they never see the kind of performance that's possible from the rest of the components in their computer.

How Much Is Enough?

It's fair to say that a PC could run with just 64MB of memory. Even with Windows XP, this would be possible (if somewhat painful). Frankly, though, I consider 256MB to be the absolute minimum if you really want to be able to do anything with your system.

You may be wondering why you need so much memory—especially for your home entertainment system PC. Basically, the answer is simple. When programs have sufficient memory to work with, they are able to load more of the program and data into memory instead of swapping stuff out to the hard drive. The less swapping that happens the better, because memory is hundreds of times faster than any hard drive.

Incidentally, certain types of applications do require more memory than others. If you guessed that video applications are real memory hogs, give yourself an A.

What Kind of Memory Should You Buy?

The type of memory you need is determined by the type of processor as well as by what the motherboard supports. The home entertainment system PC motherboard, for example, supports DDR memory. As mentioned earlier, DDR stands for double data rate, which means that this memory is able to handle data twice as fast as SDR (single data rate) memory. Most modern motherboards support either DDR or Rambus memory—the latter of which is used only with certain chipsets and Intel P4 processors.

In choosing DDR memory, you'll find that it has a rating such as PC2100, PC2700, or DDR333. These are speed ratings, and higher numbers indicate faster memory. Note, however, that PC2700 and DDR333 mean the same thing. (See www.crucial.com for more information on speed ratings.)

Buying memory that is faster than what is required for your processor and motherboard won't make your PC run any faster. Buying memory that is too slow, however, will make the system slow down or may even make it crash a lot. But even though faster memory won't speed up your system, I generally feel that the small premium you pay for faster memory is worth the cost since the faster memory has passed more stringent testing. In addition, faster memory is a good choice if you might want to upgrade to a faster processor in the future.

The Project Memory

There are a number of memory manufacturers out there, but I feel that quality is an important enough issue that I'm willing to pay a bit more to get memory I trust. As a result, I selected Crucial Technology (www.crucial.com) memory for the home entertainment system PC.

Figure 2-6 shows one of the two 512MB PC2700 DDR memory modules that I'm using for this project. With a total of 1GB of memory, the home entertainment system PC will really fly through video editing projects.

Figure 2-6
Buying quality memory, like this from Crucial Technology, is an important step in creating a stable system.

The Operating System: Windows XP

Although an operating system is not one of the basic mechanical or electronic components of a PC, it is still just as important as any of those items. Simply put, all of those other pieces are pretty useless without an operating system, since it is the software that enables the different parts of a computer to work together to create something useful.

There are several OS choices available for PCs these days, but I settled on Windows XP. There are a number of reasons for this choice:

❑ The range of application programs compatible with Windows XP is much broader than the range of application programs compatible with all non-Windows operating systems put together. If you want to be able to buy programs that you can simply install and run, you'll find the best selection (and the most reasonable prices) of professionally developed programs for Windows XP.

❑ The Macintosh OS was never a choice because it simply won't run on a PC you assemble yourself.

❑ Linux also had very limited appeal due to the difficulties involved in downloading and installing the OS, the complexity of configuring software and hardware, and the relative lack of mainstream multimedia applications.

Incidentally, I chose Windows XP Professional rather than Windows XP Home Edition due to superior networking and security components in the Professional version. If your home entertainment system PC will not be a part of your home network, Home Edition will work just as well.

Basic Options for Upgraders

If you've decided to create your home entertainment system PC by upgrading a PC you already have, you'll want to understand the options that are available to you. Generally, you need to determine which of the basic system components it makes sense to upgrade.

If you're upgrading an existing PC, you probably want to keep the case you already have. Even so, you might want to consider stripping it down by completely disassembling it and giving it a fresh coat of spray paint so that it looks a bit better in your living room. If you decide to do so, be sure to take the time to carefully mask all openings as well as each indicator—LEDs don't shine through a coat of paint very well. Before you begin painting, it's a good idea to make certain that the case is clean. Wipe it down with a soft rag that you've dampened with glass cleaner and let everything dry before you begin spraying.

While you're at it, consider if this might be a good time to upgrade that old power supply. If the old one is noisy, are you really going to want it in your home entertainment system? Besides, when you upgrade the rest of the system's components, the power demands may just be too high for the minimal unit the manufacturer installed. If you do decide to buy a new power supply, don't be tempted to buy one of the ultracheap bargain units—you can be sure they will make a lot more noise than one of the higher-priced "silent" power supplies.

If your current system has less than 256MB of memory, you already know where your next upgrade opportunity lies. Sure, you may need to toss out some of the memory that's already installed to make room for the newer, higher-capacity memory modules, but that's a small price to pay for getting better performance.

Replacing your existing processor with a faster one may be possible, but you'll have to decide for yourself if the cost is really worth it. Likewise, swapping out your motherboard may not make a lot of sense. Frankly, if your existing system runs at less than about 850 MHz, I'd suggest selling it and starting your home entertainment system PC from scratch. Ultimately, you'll be far better off and much happier with the results.

Assembling the Basic Components

Well, now that we've come this far, let's take a breather from our shopping and begin assembling the basic components. We'll get back to choosing the rest of the system soon enough. Besides, aren't you getting at least a little bit anxious about seeing the system start to take shape?

TIPS OF THE TRADE

Don't Zap Your System!

Before we begin assembling the components, I want to take just a moment to give you an important warning. The electronic components inside any computer are very susceptible to damage from static electricity. If you've ever been zapped when you touched a piece of metal or another person after walking across a carpeted floor, you've felt the effects of some pretty high-voltage static electricity. Unfortunately, it takes far less static electricity than you can feel to do major damage to computer components. To prevent this kind of damage, here are some things to keep in mind:

❑ *Don't ever work inside a PC while it is plugged in*—even if it is turned off!

❑ Always touch some metal on the case before you touch any of the other components.

❑ Leave all components in their static-resistant packaging until you absolutely must remove them, and don't handle the components any more than necessary. If you do need to set something down, set it on the static-resistant packaging to further reduce the chances of damage.

❑ Consider getting yourself a special static-reducing wristband and using it whenever you're working inside the PC. These aren't magic, though, so don't think you can ignore all of the other cautions simply because you are using the wristband.

❑ If you keep on getting shocks whenever you are in the area where you intend to assemble your PC, consider finding a different location, spraying antistatic compound on your carpeting, or buying replacements for the components you're sure to destroy.

30 MINUTES

Installing the Motherboard

Okay, so let's begin assembling our home entertainment system PC. The first step will be to mount the motherboard inside the case. This is not a difficult task, but it does require some care to avoid causing any damage. This is also the only part of the whole project where you may need to make some adjustments in order to ensure proper fit.

Preparing the I/O Panel

The first thing you need to do to prepare to install the motherboard is to prepare the I/O panel on the back of the case so that it matches the configuration of the I/O ports on the motherboard.

1. Begin by looking at the I/O ports on the motherboard, as shown in Figure 2-7.

Figure 2-7
The I/O ports on the MSI motherboard

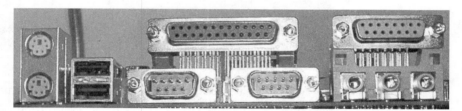

2. Next, check the I/O panel on the case. As Figure 2-8 shows, four of the knockouts have to be removed so they don't block the ports that are included on the motherboard.

Figure 2-8
You must adjust the I/O panel on the case to match the motherboard.

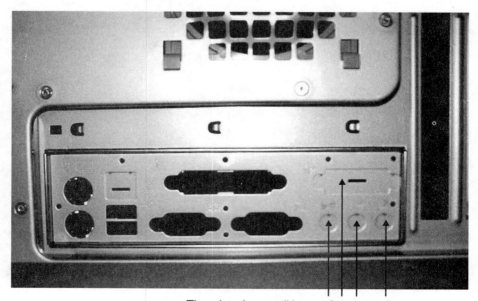

These knockouts will have to be removed.

3. The easiest way to remove the knockouts is to use a screwdriver as shown in Figure 2-9. Carefully push the knockouts in and they'll break off from the small tabs holding them in place. Be sure to remove all of the knockouts once they've fallen into the case—they would certainly be ready to short-circuit the motherboard if you left them in there.

Figure 2-9
Push out the knockouts to remove them.

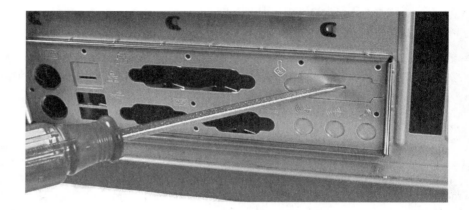

4. When you've removed the knockouts, the I/O panel should look like Figure 2-10. Now you're ready to fit the motherboard into the case.

Figure 2-10
The I/O panel should have open spaces for all of the I/O ports.

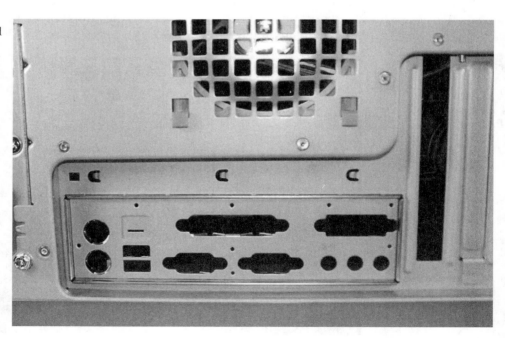

Installing the Standoffs

Next you have to install the *standoffs*—threaded metal posts that provide the mounting points for the motherboard. As Figure 2-11 shows, the Antec case comes with four standoffs already installed (as well as a number of additional standoffs in the hardware kit).

Figure 2-11
The case has threaded holes for mounting the standoffs.

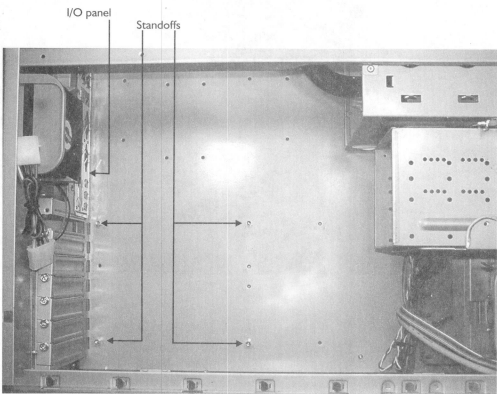

1. The case has a number of threaded holes for the standoffs, so you need to carefully examine the motherboard to determine the proper holes to use. Each of the mounting holes on the motherboard looks similar to the one shown in Figure 2-12 (note that this shows the underside of the motherboard).

Figure 2-12
Look for the correct
standoff positions.

Motherboard mounting hole

2. It turns out that the four existing standoffs in the Antec case match up
   perfectly with four of the mounting holes on the MSI motherboard; all
   we need to do is add two standoffs, as shown in Figure 2-13. (Depending
   on the case and motherboard you're using, you may not be quite as
   lucky in having so many match up and you may have to add more
   than two standoffs.)

Figure 2-13
Add or move
standoffs as
necessary to match
the motherboard.

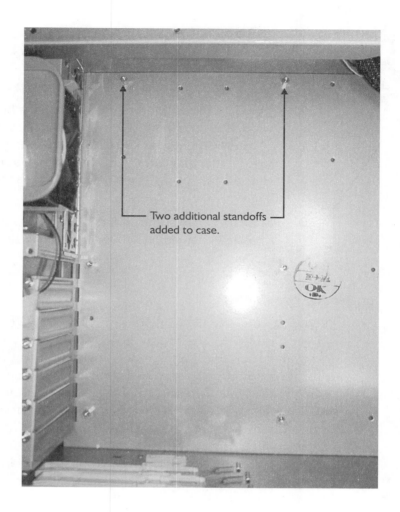

Two additional standoffs
added to case.

3. Be very careful in checking the fit of the motherboard and the standoffs. The threaded holes in the case are always located in positions that are defined by the ATX design standard, so you should be able to find the correct standoff positions without too much difficulty. Be sure to remove any standoffs that do not match motherboard mount holes, and use care so that you do not scratch any of the traces on the motherboard.

Mounting the Motherboard

Once you've tightened the standoffs into the proper threaded holes:

1. Place the motherboard into position on top of the standoffs.

2. Once all of the standoffs show through the holes, use the fine-threaded bolts from the hardware kit to fasten the motherboard in place. Don't tighten any of the bolts until you have all of them started—you may have to move the motherboard slightly to compress the spring levers near the I/O panel in order to insert all of the screws.

3. Fasten the board firmly, but don't crank the bolts down as tightly as possible. Remember, you want to hold the board in place without damaging it.

Connecting the Cables

Now that you have the motherboard installed into the case, you can connect the various cables to the motherboard. For this, you need the motherboard documentation and the case documentation so that you can determine the proper location for each of the connectors. Since each motherboard and case combination has different sets of cables, you may find yourself referring back and forth between the two frequently. At this point, it is best to take your time and make certain that you're connecting everything properly—finding and fixing a problem later will be a lot harder. Remember, you aren't in a race to get this done as quickly as possible; it's far more important to go a bit slower, refer to the manuals whenever you have a question, and do it right the first time.

Once you've connected the cables, it's time to do a little housekeeping. I strongly recommend buying a bunch of nylon cable ties and the adhesive mounting bases you use to fasten them to a surface. Then, carefully route and tie the wires so that they are out of the way. Your goal here is not only to create a very neat appearance, but also to place the cables where they won't restrict airflow. Remember, the smoother the airflow, the quieter your home entertainment system PC will run. Figure 2-14 shows how I've routed the front-panel wires along the bottom edge of the case.

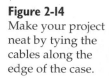

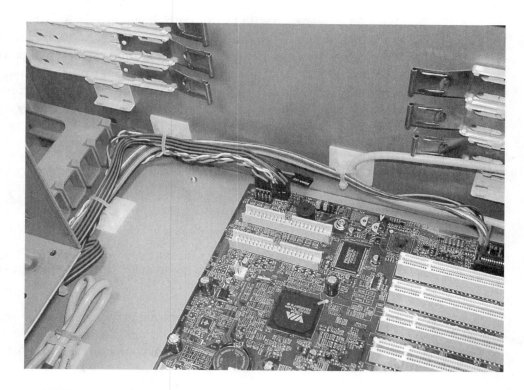

You may find that some cables simply aren't used. For example, the Antec case has cabling for a front-panel IEEE-1394 connector, but the MSI motherboard does not include an IEEE-1394 port. It's not really necessary to do anything with the extra cable except to tie it neatly out of the way. For our project, we'll be adding a video board that includes two IEEE-1394 connectors. If you choose different adapters, you may find that a video capture board you install has an internal IEEE-1394 port that you can connect to the front-panel cable.

Incidentally, there are a couple of optional brackets you can buy for the MSI motherboard. These fit into the expansion card bays at the back of the case and add some extra features. In this case, I've installed the *S bracket,* which provides some additional audio output options, including the ability to connect to a six-channel-powered speaker system for truly awesome sound output. (I discuss the S bracket more in Chapter 4.)

While we're on the subject of cables, I'll let you in on a little trick that may save you a lot of frustration. When you are connecting the front-panel USB cables, you'll notice that the connectors are set up with individual connectors for each pin rather than with the four pins being in a single connector. This provides more flexibility if you need to connect to a motherboard where the USB connectors aren't in the standard layout, but it can be a real pain trying to get all of those individual connectors onto the proper pins. To make them easier to connect, I simply lined up the individual connectors in the proper order and then taped them together to create a single inline, four-pin connector. Once that was done, it was a breeze plugging them in.

10 MINUTES ## Installing the Processor

Next we'll install the processor. Here, too, you'll want to be very careful to do everything correctly so that you avoid problems later.

Inserting the CPU in the Socket

It is, of course, very important that you insert the processor into the socket in just the right way.

1. First you should find the locating mark on the processor. Depending on the packaging, this may be a corner that is cut out or a triangular mark, as shown in Figure 2-15. This, of course, is the AMD Athlon XP processor.

Figure 2-15
The processor is marked with a triangle to indicate the proper installation direction.

2. Once you've located the positioning mark on the CPU, lift the handle on the processor socket on the motherboard, as shown in Figure 2-16. You may need to move the handle slightly sideways away from the socket before lifting it.

Figure 2-16
Open the socket by lifting the handle.

3. Next, drop the processor into the socket with the locator mark positioned so that it is next to the base of the handle. The processor should simply drop into the socket. Whatever you do, don't push it in! If it doesn't just drop into place, you either don't have it positioned properly or don't have the handle all the way up.

4. Once the CPU is in the socket, move the handle back down to the fully lowered position. Latch it under the tabs so that it stays down. Figure 2-17 shows the processor firmly seated in the socket. By the way—don't even think about turning on the power yet, because without the heat sink, the processor will be ruined immediately!

Figure 2-17
The CPU is
correctly installed.

Installing the Heat Sink

Proper heat sink installation is not difficult, but it is critical that you are very careful during the installation so that you do everything just right. It is also important that you use a heat sink that is designed and approved for your processor. For example, the TaiSol ball-bearing fan–equipped heat sink (shown earlier in Figure 2-5) is an excellent choice for AMD Athlon XP processors.

As the name implies, a heat sink is supposed to remove excess heat from the processor. To do so, it needs to make very good contact with the top of the processor. Typically this means more than simply sitting on top of the CPU—some sort of thermal interface material is also necessary. In the case of the TaiSol heat sink I'm using for the home entertainment system PC project, this material is what is known as *phase-change compound*. In Figure 2-18, the phase-change compound is the light-colored square inside the copper section on the bottom of the heat sink. Note that this heat sink comes with a plastic cover to protect the phase-change compound from damage before installation. Don't remove the plastic cover until you're ready to install the heat sink.

Figure 2-18
The TaiSol heat
sink is set up for
maximum heat
transfer from
the CPU.

Phase-change —
compound

AMD advises against using standard heat transfer grease. Unfortunately, the
phase-change compound is a one-time–use product, which means that it must be
replaced each time you remove the heat sink. If you have problems finding the
correct material, you may want to check the AMD web site (www.amd.com) for
recommended products. I've found that getting the correct material can be a
little difficult, so I avoid removing the heat sink unless absolutely necessary.

To install the heat sink:

1. Carefully place it over the CPU, which is already installed in the socket.
   The step you saw on the heat sink bottom in Figure 2-18 sits over the
   raised hinge section of the socket (the pivot for the handle).

2. On two sides of the heat sink, you'll see a spring clip as shown in
   Figure 2-19. The spring clip should line up with the tabs on the CPU
   socket. When everything is perfectly aligned, use a small screwdriver
   (see Figure 2-19) to push the clip out and down over the tabs. It's
   probably best to clip the side nearest the power supply first since
   there's so little room to work on that side. (Remember, though, that
   if you've selected a different CPU and fan combination, you'll need
   to follow the directions that came with them to make sure you install
   everything properly.)

Figure 2-19
Carefully hook the
spring clip over
the tabs with a
small screwdriver.

3. Once you have installed the clip on one side, repeat the process on the
   other side. Figure 2-20 shows a close-up view of the spring clip
   properly seated over the socket tabs.

Figure 2-20
The spring clips on
both sides must be
fully seated like this.

4. When you've verified that the spring clip is in place, plug the heat sink fan power lead into the fan power next to the memory slots, as shown in Figure 2-21. The connector is keyed so that it can only be installed in the proper direction.

Figure 2-21
Don't forget to plug in the fan power connector.

5 MINUTES

Installing the Memory

We're down to the final basic components that we'll install in this chapter—the memory modules. Although the MSI motherboard has three memory slots, we're only going to use two of them to hold our 1GB of PC2700 DDR memory from Crucial Technology. That way, we'll have an open slot in the event we decide to upgrade our memory in the future.

Memory modules are keyed so they will fit into the memory slots in only one direction (refer to Figure 2-6). To install a memory module:

1. Make certain the handles at each end of the slot are pushed out all the way.

2. Next, insert the memory module straight into the slot, as shown in Figure 2-22.

Figure 2-22
Don't rock the
memory modules
as you insert them.

As you push the memory module straight down, the handle will swing up into place, as shown in Figure 2-23. Once the memory is fully seated, the handle will snap into position next to the memory module. Both handles must be right up next to the memory module.

Figure 2-23
The handles will
move into place
as you seat the
memory module.

3. Make certain that you have fully seated the first memory module and
then insert the second one. Figure 2-24 shows both memory modules
installed in the home entertainment system PC.

Figure 2-24
The memory modules
are properly installed
and ready to use.

Although I did specify the Windows XP operating system as one of the basic
system components, we'll have to wait to install it until we've added some
additional components to our PC. In the next chapter, we'll look at some options
for one very important part of the home entertainment system PC—the video
components.

At this point, you should double-check to make certain the following items have been completed:

❑ The motherboard is fastened into the case. Remember to make sure that you removed the I/O panel knockouts that were covering several items.

❑ The processor is properly installed on the motherboard. Make certain that the heat sink is correctly installed and its fan is connected to the fan connector on the motherboard.

❑ The power connector has been plugged in to the motherboard.

❑ The memory modules are fully seated in the memory sockets.

Chapter 3
Selecting a Video System

Tools of the Trade

To complete this chapter you'll need:

ATI All-In-Wonder Radeon 8500DV video card

Terk TV5 amplified indoor TV antenna

Terk Leapfrog WaveMaster 20 home broadcast system

Planar PL201M-BK LCD monitor

In this chapter, we consider your video system options for the home entertainment system PC. It is in choosing the video components that we'll find some of the most striking differences between the needs of this project and what is included in the average home PC. For example, for the home entertainment system PC, we'll want to have the following capabilities, which are still not very common on most systems:

- ❏ **TV out capability**   Enables you to view DVD movies, TV shows, and video games on a big screen television.

- ❏ **TV tuner**   Enables you to view and record TV shows. This also includes such handy features as the ability to pause live TV and to cut out the commercials during playback.

- ❏ **Video capture capabilities**   Enables you to create your own video productions using your digital camcorder or even your analog VCR.

- ❏ **Remote control**   Enables you to control the TV functions without getting up from the sofa (or maybe even from another part of the house).

You may not expect these features in a PC, but as you'll see in this chapter, getting them is simply a matter of finding and buying the correct pieces. For those of you who are still in upgrade mode rather than build-from-scratch mode, I'll show you a couple of ways to add most of these capabilities to your existing PC. In fact, I'm even going to show you one cool product that will bring TV to your PC without even requiring you to open up the case!

I'll finish off the chapter by showing you a few very useful accessories to complement your home entertainment system PC. Although these accessories are not a part of the PC itself, they are very handy.

Choosing a Video Adapter

Choosing a video adapter can be pretty confusing. There are many different choices and few really understandable guides to making your selection. When you throw in the special requirements we've laid out for the home entertainment system PC, it's even more confusing, since pinpointing which video adapters actually have all the features we want is often difficult. In this section, we look at those requirements a little more closely to see how they really affect our choices.

AGP vs. PCI Video Adapters

High-performance video requires an awful lot of data to be transferred between your PC and your monitor. All of that data must pass through the video adapter, which means that the interface between the video adapter and the rest of the system must be capable of moving a lot of information very quickly.

Most of the expansion slots on modern PCs are *Peripheral Component Interconnect (PCI)* slots. The PCI bus is capable of fairly high data rates, but it's not really fast enough to feed the data to a high-performance video adapter. Because of this, a special video connection—the *Accelerated Graphics Port (AGP)*—was developed. Nearly all motherboards now include an AGP slot specifically for video adapters. Figure 3-1 shows the AGP and PCI connectors on the home entertainment system PC motherboard. The AGP connector is always located closest to the CPU on the motherboard. One reason for this is to make the path between the CPU and the video card as short as possible. Also, there is never more than one AGP connector, but there are usually several PCI connectors.

Figure 3-1
The AGP connector
allows you to use a
higher-performance
video adapter.

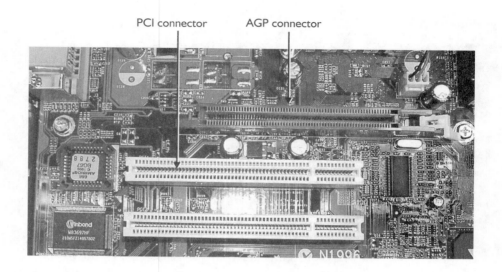

PCI connector   AGP connector

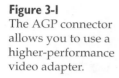

Figure 3-1
The AGP connector
allows you to use a
higher-performance
video adapter.

Even though the AGP bus was a lot faster than the PCI bus, the capabilities of video adapters soon outstripped what even the standard AGP bus could deliver. That's why you'll soon see that AGP slots (and video adapters) are now generally rated as AGP 2X or AGP 4X—depending on whether they are two or four times the capacity of the original AGP bus. Faster is better, of course, so we'll be looking for a video adapter that fits into the AGP slot and is rated at 4X (since this is supported by the home entertainment system PC motherboard from MSI).

You may also see AGP 8X being mentioned, but few motherboards and video adapters support that speed. In addition, the other features we need for the home entertainment system PC, such as the TV tuner, are only available on 2X or 4X boards.

Video Capture

Another important function of the home entertainment system PC is the ability to capture video signals from both analog and digital sources. This enables you to view, save, and edit videos of many different types. For example, you might want to use footage that you've recorded with your digital camcorder to create a home movie. You might also want to transfer an old video tape of family members to the more modern DVD format so that it can easily be shared with future generations. Regardless of the source, you can only do these things if you have a method of getting the video data into your PC.

TIPS OF THE TRADE

Getting the Correct Video Input

Analog and digital video signals need separate types of input ports. Analog video is typically supplied as either an RF (*radio frequency*) or a *composite* video signal. A little less common is an *S-Video* signal (which is actually pretty closely related to composite video). S-Video provides a higher-quality video signal than does composite video. Although these terms may not be familiar to you, you've probably used analog video signals many times without realizing it. If you have an antenna or a cable TV connection connected to your TV, you've been using an analog TV signal. The typical push-on coax cable is used when the video signal is RF. If your TV is connected to your VCR, you may be using a different type of cable that connects via an RCA—or *cinch*—jack (usually this jack is yellow). In this case, you would be using an analog composite video signal.

Digital video is stored as data that a computer can process. The newer digital camcorders and some high-end digital cameras use an IEEE-1394 connection to send video to a PC. This type of connection is also known as FireWire or iLink, and is also used for external hard drives as well as to connect Sony PlayStation 2 video game consoles together. Figure 3-2 shows a video card input bracket with both an RF and an IEEE-1394 connector. The other connectors on this bracket are used for connecting to a monitor and to a special external connector.

Figure 3-2
This video card can capture both digital and analog video signals.

Digital (IEEE-1394) input   Analog (RF) input

As you will see a bit later, this same video card has an external connecting block with composite video inputs and outputs as well.

Video cards are not the only method of capturing video on a PC. There are also separate video capture cards as well as separate TV tuner cards. Indeed, if you are upgrading an existing PC rather than building the home entertainment system PC from scratch, you may find that these separate cards fit your needs better than a new video card that combines all of these functions on a single card.

TV Out

The next important feature we'll want for our home entertainment system PC is the ability to output a signal to a TV. You probably would prefer watching DVD movies and TV shows on a big screen TV rather than on your average computer monitor, and you probably don't want a monitor sitting next to your TV anyway. With the TV out feature, you can even use your TV as a monitor, although the very nature of television sets means that you'll be limited to a lower resolution than you are accustomed to seeing on your monitor—the picture will be larger, but you'll see far fewer pixels.

The TV out feature is generally available in two different formats—composite video and S-Video. You'll want to use the S-Video output if your TV supports this. Composite video has slightly lower video quality since all the video signals are combined in a single wire rather than each having its own wire. Figure 3-3 shows the output connectors that are available with the video card we'll be using for the home entertainment system PC.

Figure 3-3
You need TV out to send your video signals to your TV set.

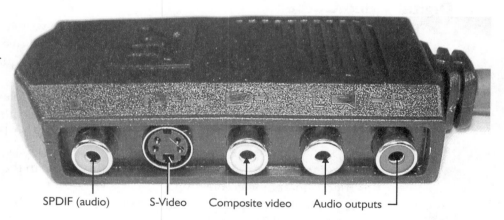

SPDIF (audio)   S-Video   Composite video   Audio outputs

As Figure 3-3 shows, the output box also includes an *SPDIF* (Sony/Philips Digital Interface) jack and two analog audio output jacks. These can be used to connect to an audio amplifier in your home entertainment system (although we'll be using the six-channel audio output features included on the MSI motherboard).

TIPS OF THE TRADE

Playing Games

Before we go too far off the deep end with all of this television coverage, let's not forget that another important part of our home entertainment system PC is its video game support. After all, what better place could there be to play some video games than sitting on your living room sofa?

From a video card standpoint, probably the most important feature for gaming is high-end graphics power. We need a video board that can easily handle 3-D graphics and that has enough memory to render our games at a high resolution. The video board I have selected for the home entertainment system PC project will easily fill these needs. In fact, it even includes several games within the box, so you can begin playing as soon as you have finished assembling the home entertainment system PC.

Digital Video Output

Depending on the type of monitor you use, it may be very handy to get a video card that has *DVI-I*—digital video output for flat panel displays. This type of output can greatly enhance the picture you see on a high-quality liquid crystal display (LCD) monitor.

Standard cathode-ray tube (CRT) monitors (as well as televisions) are analog devices. Your computer, of course, is a digital device. This means that the digital video signal that is generated by your video board must be converted to an analog signal before it is sent out through the VGA port to your monitor. As you can imagine, a certain amount of display quality is lost in the process of making this digital-to-analog conversion.

LCD monitors are inherently digital devices, so if they have the proper DVI-I interface (not all LCD monitors do), they can use the digital signal from a DVI-I-equipped video card, and no digital-to-analog (and back to digital) conversion is necessary. As a result, the image quality does not suffer from unnecessary conversions.

Consider Your Future Video Needs

Some video cards (including the one I've selected for this project) have the ability to output the video signal as DVI-I as well as to convert to a standard VGA analog signal if necessary. If you think you might want to buy an LCD monitor at some point, you may want to consider buying a video card that offers DVI-I output.

Choosing a TV Tuner Card

An important part of any home entertainment center is the television. To fully integrate our PC into our home entertainment center, we need to incorporate TV viewing capabilities within the PC. We do this by adding a TV tuner card. As you can imagine, there are several options in TV tuner cards. Let's take a look at a couple of different examples.

Stand-alone TV Tuner Cards

The stand-alone TV tuner card enables your PC to act as a television set. It also enables you to record your favorite TV shows, as well as to pause live TV. Actually, all the TV tuners we will discuss incorporate this type of feature, known as a *personal video recorder (PVR)*. Figure 3-4 shows one of the more popular stand-alone TV tuner cards, the Pinnacle PCTV (www.pinnaclesys.com).

Figure 3-4
Stand-alone TV tuner cards add TV reception to your PC.

One feature that makes this card stand out compared to other stand-alone TV tuner cards is the infrared remote that is included (see Figure 3-5). Obviously, this is an important feature for our home entertainment system PC. If you buy a different stand-alone TV tuner card, you'll probably find that you need to use the PC keyboard to control the TV tuner functions. The remote control just seems a whole lot more convenient when it comes to controlling your TV watching.

Figure 3-5
The Pinnacle PCTV includes this handy remote control.

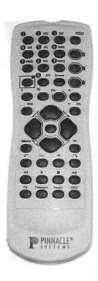

The Pinnacle PCTV card also would be an excellent choice if you have decided to upgrade an existing PC rather than building a home entertainment system PC from scratch. You need one open PCI slot to install this card.

Integrated TV Tuner/Video Cards

Integrated TV tuner/video cards serve the dual purpose of being a TV tuner and the video card all in one. Figure 3-6 shows an example of the ATI All-In-Wonder Radeon 8500DV (www.ati.com). This card incorporates all the features of the stand-alone TV tuner cards, including the ability to pause live TV.

Figure 3-6
The ATI
All-In-Wonder
Radeon 8500DV
is a complete TV
tuner/video card
in one.

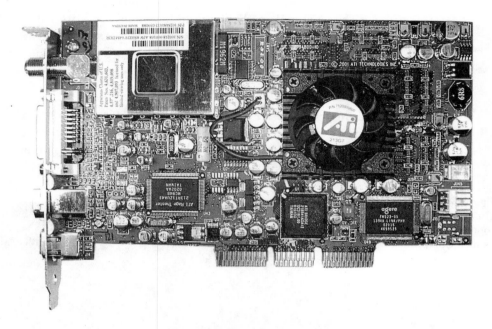

As Figure 3-7 shows, the ATI All-In-Wonder Radeon 8500DV also includes a remote control. Unlike the Pinnacle PCTV remote, the ATI remote control is an RF remote, which means that you will be able to control the TV tuner in your home entertainment system PC from up to 100 feet away from the PC. This will be especially handy if your home entertainment system PC is not located in the same room as your big screen TV. I'll show you a way to broadcast the TV signal a distance from your PC a bit later in this chapter.

Figure 3-7
The ATI
All-In-Wonder
Radeon 8500DV
remote control
uses RF signals for
greater distance.

The ATI All-In-Wonder Radeon 8500DV fits into the AGP slot on the motherboard, and since you do not need a separate slot for a TV tuner card, all of your PCI slots are available for other types of expansion cards.

External TV Tuners

This next type of TV tuner is unique in that it does not need to be installed within your PC. Rather, it connects to your PC using a USB port. The Pinnacle Bungee DVD, shown in Figure 3-8, is the only PC TV tuner product of its type (www.pinnaclesys.com).

Figure 3-8
This TV tuner connects to your PC using a USB port.

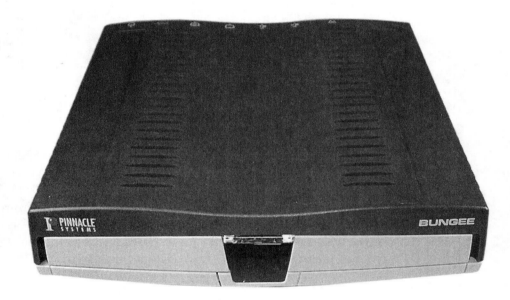

As you can imagine, the Pinnacle Bungee DVD would be an excellent choice for someone who wanted to upgrade an existing PC for use in their home entertainment system. What you might not have considered is that this unit can also be used with a laptop PC, something that is not possible with any of the other TV tuner cards.

HEADS UP!

But There's No Remote...

The one shortcoming of the Pinnacle Bungee DVD is its lack of a remote control. Still, the fact that you don't even need to open your PC to use the Pinnacle Bungee DVD is a very appealing feature.

Installing the Project Video Card

With all of the excellent choices available, it was a little difficult settling on the best video card and TV tuner card for the home entertainment system PC. In the end, the combination of a video card and TV tuner card together on one card in the ATI All-In-Wonder Radeon 8500DV makes it the winner. Not only does this card offer a lot of function in one slot, but it includes an excellent software bundle. In addition, this particular model includes the IEEE-1394 port for digital video input. ATI also makes a version of this card without the IEEE-1394 port, but even if you don't have a digital camcorder yet, consider that you may want to get one in the future, and having the 1394 port already available will make things a lot handier.

Finally, the fact that the ATI All-In-Wonder Radeon 8500DV remote control is an RF remote really adds a major bit of convenience. Even if your home entertainment system PC is located in your living room, the RF remote is simply handier than an infrared remote because it doesn't need to be pointed in a particular direction in order to work.

Installing the video card is quite simple:

1. The AGP slot is always the one closest to the CPU. This slot is also a different color and shape than the PCI slots. Figure 3-9 shows the proper method of inserting the video card. Make certain that you push straight down without rocking the card. You may need to use two hands to insert the card correctly and push it all the way in.

Figure 3-9
Push on both ends of the card to install it.

2. AGP slots have a small tab similar to the one at each end of the memory slots. Figure 3-10 shows how this tab moves up into place once the video card is fully seated. Although it may be tempting, don't use your finger to raise the tab. Rather, push down firmly on the video card, and when it is fully seated, the tab will come up on its own. This gives you a clear visual indication that the board is installed properly.

Figure 3-10
This tab indicates that the card is fully seated when the tab is all the way up.

This tab moves all the way up when the video card is fully seated.

3. Once the video card is firmly seated, make sure that you insert a screw into the bracket to hold the video card in place. The hardware kit included with the Antec case includes the proper screws.

Some Video Extras

This section shows you a couple of accessories that you may find very useful with your home entertainment system PC. Although these accessories may not be necessary in your particular situation, I find them to be very handy in the ways that they extend the capabilities of the home entertainment system PC.

An Amplified Antenna

If you want to watch over-the-air TV, you will quickly find that TV tuner cards require an external antenna. Not only that, but in most cases that external antenna will have to be an amplified antenna in order to produce enough signal strength to provide a decent-quality picture.

Since we want our home entertainment system PC not only to work as well as possible but also to look good, a set of "rabbit ears" simply isn't going to make the grade. Rather, we'll want something like the Terk TV5 amplified indoor TV antenna, shown in Figure 3-11 (www.terk.com).

Figure 3-11
This Terk TV5 antenna provides the signal strength our TV tuner card needs.

Not only does this Terk TV5 amplified indoor TV antenna look good, but it also includes a secondary video input and input selector switch. As a result, you can easily hook up another video source, such as a satellite TV receiver, a VCR, or even a video game console. Who says that things have to look ugly to be really useful?

An Audio and Video Broadcast System

Another accessory that you may find very useful is an audio and video broadcast system. This enables you to send the audio and video signals from the home entertainment system PC to a different room in your house. This is especially handy if you don't want to place the home entertainment system PC in your living room, but you still want to be able to watch DVD movies or listen to music in your living room.

Figure 3-12 shows the accessory that makes this possible. It is the Terk Leapfrog WaveMaster 20 home broadcast system (www.terk.com). This unit operates on a 2.4 GHz transmitter/receiver system so that your home entertainment system PC can be as much as 100 feet away from your TV. A single receiver comes in the package, but you can add receivers so that you can view the video or listen to audio in several different rooms.

Figure 3-12
This transmitter/
receiver system
enables you to
broadcast your audio
and video throughout
your home.

Installing the Terk Leapfrog WaveMaster 20 home broadcast system couldn't
be easier. You simply plug in the audio and video connectors, plug in each power
supply, aim the antennas, and watch. It sure beats stringing a bunch of cables all
over the place!

Large LCD Display

Okay, so this next option probably isn't for everyone. Quite honestly, large
LCD displays are still considerably more expensive than CRT monitors. In
fact, the cost of a 23.1-inch LCD display is probably at least equal to a 45-inch
big screen TV.

So why would anyone want to buy a large LCD monitor for the home
entertainment system PC when they can easily hook up a big screen TV and use it
for the display? I can think of a number of very good reasons:

❏ If you intend to use the home entertainment system PC as more than
just a home entertainment center, you'll definitely want something
with much higher resolution than a TV for those times when you're
using the system as a computer.

❏ If you have limited space, such as in an apartment, you may not have
room for a big screen TV. A large LCD display also takes far less room
than a standard PC monitor, so you can fit in a larger LCD display
and really enjoy watching your DVD movies and favorite TV shows.

❑ Frankly, a big LCD display is just a lot more impressive looking than any TV or CRT monitor could ever hope to be. One look at the Planar PL201M-BK (www.planar.com), shown in Figure 3-13, should convince you of that. This happens to be a fairly economical 20.1-inch display— Planar also offers a 23.1-inch model that will easily fulfill all of your home entertainment system PC video needs.

Figure 3-13
This Planar LCD display is the ultimate home entertainment system PC option.

A Video Card for Upgraders

Finally, if you're upgrading an existing system (or if you prefer to keep your video card and TV tuner card as separate components), you may want to consider a video card like the XFX GeForce4 Ti4200 (www.xfxgraphics.com), shown in Figure 3-14. This video card offers an unbeatable combination of nVIDIA graphics power along with very competitive pricing. It has DVI-I output, so it will work with your digital LCD display, and it also includes S-Video output for connection to a big screen TV. This is also a great choice for playing video games on your home entertainment system PC.

Figure 3-14
For a stand-alone high-performance video card at a bargain price, you will want to consider this board from XFX Graphics.

Well, now that our video options are in place, it's time to take a look at our audio options. Even though the home entertainment system PC motherboard includes excellent onboard audio capabilities, Chapter 4 presents some additional items we may want to consider.

TESTING 1-2-3

At this point, you should double-check to make certain the following items have been completed:

❑ The video card is fully seated in the AGP slot. It is easy to have a problem here, so double-check to make sure it's securely in place.

❑ The video input/output box is connected. You may want to use the included adhesive material to fasten it to the top or side of the case.

Chapter 4

Choosing Your Audio System

Tools of the Trade

To complete this chapter you'll need:

The S bracket for the MSI KT3 Ultra2-R series motherboard

Altec Lansing model 5100 system

You'll probably be listening to your home entertainment system PC more than you'll be watching videos. After all, we're setting up a system that not only can serve up video entertainment but also has complete audio features. Because of this, I'm going to use this chapter to discuss some of your audio system options.

If you're adding the home entertainment system PC to an existing home entertainment center, you may already have a number of audio components that will fill the bill quite nicely. Even so, it's entirely possible that you'll find that the advanced audio features we're adding to the home entertainment system PC may call for some upgrades of some of your existing components. For example, if you've been putting off updating your old two-speaker stereo system, you will probably be very pleasantly surprised by how much more lifelike DVD movies seem when you add the necessary speakers to produce surround sound. In many ways, the difference is almost as spectacular as going from listening to music on a monaural AM radio to listening to stereo CDs.

So let's begin looking at selecting the audio components for our home entertainment system PC.

Selecting Sound Output Options

The sound capabilities of virtually all modern PCs are actually pretty good. It's very rare to find a PC that doesn't have at least some sound capabilities built in. This makes our task of selecting sound options for the home entertainment system PC a fairly easy one. Primarily, we'll be looking for the extra features that will make our system stand out.

There are two ways to provide sound capabilities for modern PCs. The first, and most traditional, is to add a sound card. The second is to use a motherboard that already has the sound features built into it. Both approaches offer certain advantages:

❏ A stand-alone sound card may offer additional features compared to an onboard sound chipset.

❏ Built-in sound capabilities are generally less expensive than a quality stand-alone sound card.

❏ In some cases, a sound card promises to provide superior-quality sound, although this is far less true now than it was in the past.

In either case, the most important factor in choosing the audio source for your home entertainment system PC is how it sounds. You can just as easily end up with poor-quality sound from a sound card as from onboard sound if you aren't careful in making your selection. Fortunately, it seems as though good-quality sound is becoming both more common and more affordable.

Let's take a look at the features you'll want from whichever sound option you choose for your home entertainment system PC.

Features to Look For

It's a given that you'll want good sound. Unfortunately, you probably won't be able to try out the exact combination of components that you'll be using before you buy. Even if you happen to shop at a store that has some demo machines on display, you aren't likely to discover one of them that is configured exactly like your home entertainment system PC. So, you're left with choosing your sound options based on the features they offer as well as the recommendations of other people who have tried out these same components.

At the very least, you will find that most every PC sound card (or onboard sound system) offers certain basic features. These include:

❏ Stereo sound output suitable for amplified speakers or connecting to an external amplifier

❏ Line-in input

❏ Microphone input

Figure 4-1 shows the typical layout of the sound ports.

Figure 4-1
Typical sound ports as found on most modern PCs

Speaker out   Line in   Mic in

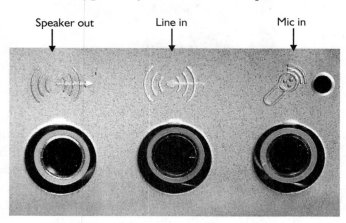

When you step up from the basics, you will find that your sound options may include some additional handy features, which we'll look at next.

Dolby 5.1

Years ago, all sound reproduction was monaural. Stereo came along to provide a much more lifelike sound experience. With stereo sound, you could tell the source of a sound just by listening. As an example of this, consider what happens when you are watching a movie in a theater. If you hear an off-camera voice, you can tell whether the unseen actor is to the right or the left of the screen from the position of the sound.

In real life, sounds come from all directions—not just from the right or left. This is the idea behind Dolby 5.1 surround sound. This type of sound system uses a number of different speakers to produce true positional sound. Dolby 5.1 is often an option on better PC sound cards. One reason for this is that DVD movies often use Dolby 5.1 surround sound.

For the best Dolby 5.1 surround sound, you need a speaker system with at least six different speaker enclosures (remember that some speaker enclosures include more than one speaker in the enclosure). These speakers are typically called front right, front left, rear right, rear left, center, and subwoofer. This speaker arrangement presents a problem, since the typical PC sound port arrangement has a single stereo output (speaker out) port—enough to drive just two of the six Dolby 5.1 surround sound speakers. In other words, there simply isn't any way to drive the remaining four speakers.

Figure 4-2 shows one possible solution to this dilemma—the optional S bracket you can buy for the MSI KT3 Ultra2-R series motherboard we've selected for this project. This bracket provides several additional output ports. The two miniature stereo jacks provide center channel/subwoofer output from one jack, and rear speaker output from the other.

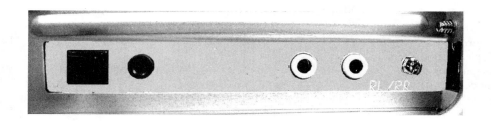

Even if you do not add the S bracket to your system, you can configure the MSI motherboard for six-channel output. Unfortunately, doing so precludes use of the line in and mic in ports on the back of your PC for their normal function, since their jacks must then be used to drive the extra four speaker channels. Even so, the MSI motherboard does have additional front-panel sound port connections you could use to regain this functionality.

TIPS OF
THE TRADE

Identify Your Outputs

If you buy a sound card with Dolby 5.1 output, you'll find a variety of port options. Some sound cards take the approach of disabling the line in and mic in ports so they can be used for the extra speaker channels, some include a separate output block you can mount on the front of your PC, and some only provide Dolby 5.1 output through a digital connection—which requires the use of a separate Dolby 5.1 amplifier and precludes the use of powered Dolby 5.1 speaker systems. Be prepared to ask a lot of questions before you buy so you don't end up with a sound card that offers a feature but makes it impossible for you to take advantage of the feature!

Digital Out

One of the biggest problems with multichannel sound is simply that it takes so many wires to transmit the necessary signals. As you saw in the previous section, you need to use at least three stereo jacks just to output the sound signals from your home entertainment system PC to a set of powered speakers. Now imagine how confusing (and messy) everything will be if you decide that you want to connect the outputs from your home entertainment system PC to the inputs on a component receiver in your home entertainment center so that you can take advantage of your existing speakers.

Audio component manufacturers figured out some time ago that it just wasn't practical to expect the average user to be able to correctly connect a whole bunch of different units together using a huge number of different cables. The chances for error were just too high and the proliferation of ugly wires running all over the place simply didn't appeal to most people. There had to be a better way to send multichannel signals between the different components.

In a rare instance of competing manufacturers agreeing to a standard that allows different brands of equipment to function properly together (rather than sticking with proprietary solutions), two types of digital signal connections were developed. One uses fiber-optic cables and the other uses coaxial cables. Although the two are certainly incompatible with each other, both provide a digital pathway for multichannel signals to be transmitted between audio components using a single cable.

It's rare today to find a quality home entertainment center receiver that does not offer a digital optical input, a digital coax input, or both. Most units seem to have a total of at least three such inputs so that they can accept digital audio input from several different sources.

If you want to connect your home entertainment system PC to one of these receivers and have multichannel sound, you'll need to provide a digital audio output on your PC. As Figure 4-2 showed, the MSI S bracket has both a digital optical and a digital coax output port. If you decide to use a stand-alone audio card, you'll want to look for one with a digital output port that is compatible with whichever type is available on your receiver.

Put Your Sound Options into Perspective

It is, of course, always important to keep things in the proper perspective. Although you may want Dolby 5.1 surround sound for full effect when watching DVD movies and playing certain video games, for simply listening to music, stereo sound is really all that you need. The MP3s or other audio files you record onto your home entertainment system PC will be in stereo—not Dolby 5.1 surround sound. If your goal is to use your home entertainment system PC primarily as a virtually unlimited music jukebox and you don't care about using it for playing DVDs, you probably don't need a digital audio output (for now, anyway).

Front-Panel Sound Ports

Since you're building your own home entertainment system PC, why not make things as convenient as possible? If you've ever tried to connect a set of stereo headphones or a microphone to the audio connectors on the back of the PC, you know how inconvenient this can be. A set of front-panel audio jacks would sure make things a whole lot easier. You could simply plug things in as needed, and remove them when they're in the way.

Watch for Front-Panel Options

Few stand-alone sound cards support front-panel audio jacks. There are exceptions, of course, so if this feature interests you, you'll want to add it to your list of things to watch for when you go shopping.

Not surprisingly, the multitalented MSI motherboard that is the basis for your home entertainment system PC does offer you the option of front-panel audio jacks (using connector JAUD1 on the motherboard—see Figure 4-3). By connecting the proper cables to the motherboard connector, you can have a mic jack and a stereo headphone jack that you can place wherever you like on the front panel. By the way, in Figure 4-3, the JAUD1 connector is shown in the default configuration with two jumpers in place. These jumpers must be installed if you do not use front-panel audio but want the line in jack on the back panel to be functional.

Figure 4-3
The JAUD1 connector on the MSI motherboard provides for front-panel audio jacks.

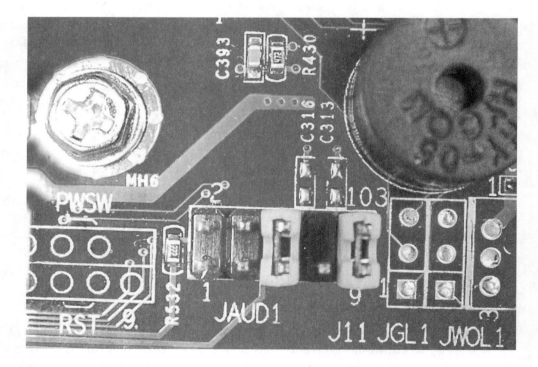

Note, however, that you're on your own in figuring out a mounting arrangement for any front-panel audio jacks you decide to add. The Antec case does not have a dedicated set of front-panel audio jacks. Personally, I would probably use one of the removable plates (such as the one we'll need to remove to add a floppy disk drive in Chapter 5) as the mounting location. You'll need to carefully drill the plate and run the audio cables to the motherboard connector, but if you've made it this far in assembling your home entertainment system PC, you won't have any trouble with this optional part of the project. Just be careful not to damage anything important while you're drilling the plate as you make holes to mount the jacks!

Choosing a Stand-alone Sound Card

If you're upgrading an existing PC or if you've decided you'd rather use a stand-alone sound card instead of the built-in sound capabilities included on the MSI motherboard, you'll have a number of reasonable choices. Various companies such as Turtle Beach, Creative, and Guillemot all produce some very good sound cards. So the question is, how do you select the best one for your needs? Let's take a look at some things you'll want to consider:

❑ Most PC sound cards only offer stereo sound output, so you can scratch them from your list if you want Dolby 5.1 surround sound when you're watching your favorite DVD movies. Look for the capability of driving a six-speaker system if you want to really enjoy the sound from your home entertainment system PC.

❑ A few sound cards offer various audio connections that are easily reachable from the front of your PC through either an external connection box or by means of a front-panel plate that fits into an empty drive bay. If you want easy access to a mic jack or a stereo headset jack, this could be important to you. Try to get a look at the external connection box before you buy, though—some of them are pretty clunky looking.

❑ Manufacturers sometimes tout the number of voices, or synthesizer channels, that are included on their sound cards. This is essentially a worthless measurement for anyone except a musician since it only applies to MIDI (Musical Instrument Digital Interface) music, and has absolutely nothing whatsoever to do with playback of audio CDs, MP3s, or DVD movies.

❑ Digital audio output is still fairly uncommon on most PC sound cards, but if you're thinking of connecting your home entertainment system PC to a high-quality home entertainment center receiver that offers digital audio inputs, this is another thing to watch for. You may want to add this to your list of desirable features even if you aren't planning on connecting to a receiver right away. Who knows if you might change your mind at some point in the future? If you do, you'll be glad you took the extra effort to include this feature now.

Installing Your Sound Options

Since the solution chosen for the home entertainment system PC is to use the onboard sound capabilities of the MSI motherboard, installation is a snap. In fact, unless you choose to add the S bracket or front-panel audio, there is no additional installation required.

If you have decided on a stand-alone sound card for your home entertainment system PC, you'll find that the installation isn't much harder. You simply insert the sound card into one of the PCI slots on the motherboard and fasten it in place with the screw you removed when you removed the blank plate.

In either case, connecting your speakers is also pretty straightforward. Note, however, that you may have to enable six-channel sound using a setup utility (such as the one included with the MSI motherboard). If so, this step will have to wait until you have completed the assembly of your entire system.

Audio Amplification Recommendations

The output from a PC sound card is at a fairly low level and won't produce very much volume unless some additional amplification is applied. In most cases, this additional amplification is provided by powered speakers. You can, however, also connect to your home entertainment center receiver. The choice really comes down to personal preference and the existing components in your home entertainment center.

Connecting to Your Existing Audio System

If you already have a high-quality audio system, you may want to more fully integrate the home entertainment system PC into that system by connecting the audio outputs from the PC to your existing system. The method you use depends on the audio output capabilities both of your PC and of your existing audio system.

If either your PC or your existing audio system is limited to two channels—stereo—your hookup choices are fairly simple. In virtually every case, the audio output jacks on a PC are known as 1/8-inch (3.5mm) miniature stereo jacks. On the other hand, the audio input jacks on typical stereo receiver are different—RCA (or cinch) jacks. Fortunately, this does not present a real problem. To connect the two, you simply need to buy an adapter cable like the one shown in Figure 4-4.

Figure 4-4
Use an adapter
cable like this one
to connect your
PC audio output
to your receiver.

If both your PC and your existing audio system have Dolby 5.1 digital audio, you can simply get the proper fiber-optic or coax cable to connect the two. As mentioned earlier, make certain to check which type of digital audio connection is available at both ends of the connection. Remember, fiber-optic and coax are incompatible with each other.

Label Your Cables

Regardless of which method you use to connect the audio output from your PC to the audio input on your home entertainment center receiver, make certain that you label the ends of the cable to clearly indicate its purpose. In fact, labeling all of your cables is an excellent idea that will save you much frustration in the future.

Buying a New Amplifier

If your existing receiver is several years old, it probably lacks some modern features such as Dolby 5.1 surround sound. Although this won't really affect the sound quality when playing music, it does mean that you'll be missing out on a lot of the sounds when you play DVD movies. After all, isn't the whole idea here to get the most entertainment possible from your home entertainment system PC? Maybe it's time to upgrade that old receiver with a multichannel unit with a few more bells and whistles.

The real question you have to ask yourself, however, is whether you're ready to buy not only a new audio receiver but also the additional speakers you'll need for Dolby 5.1 surround sound. Not only that, but you're going to have to try and find room for all those new speakers, plus run the wires for them too.

Speaker System Options

If you haven't been shopping for speakers for some time, you may be surprised at just how much sound the manufacturers are able to cram into some awfully tiny packages. This isn't a case of speaker designers suddenly learning new ways to defy the laws of physics, it's just that modern materials and computer-aided design have enabled them to accomplish far more than ever before in producing big sound from little speakers.

Understanding Speaker Systems and Sounds

It's important to understand a few points about how we hear and perceive sounds. The typical human is able to hear sounds in the range from about 20 Hz to a bit short of 20 KHz. Human speech generally falls into a range from about 1 KHz to about 4 KHz. Our ears can tell the direction of high-frequency sounds far better than they can determine where low-frequency sounds originate.

Putting all of this information together, it's easy to see why six-speaker sound systems work so well:

❑ The subwoofer only reproduces low frequencies. Since it's hard for us to determine where low-frequency sounds are coming from, a single subwoofer can handle all of the low-frequency sounds without really affecting our listening experience. This also means that the subwoofer can be located pretty much anywhere.

❑ The center channel speaker handles most of the midfrequency sounds. Since this covers the range of human speech, voices seem to come mostly from right in front of us—which is where most speech probably originates in a typical movie anyway. This makes it easier for you to understand what the actors are saying.

❑ The four satellite speakers—front right, front left, rear right, and rear left—reproduce primarily high frequencies. Since these are the frequencies that enable us to determine the direction of sounds, placing these speakers well out from the center speaker greatly enhances the effect of positional sound. As an added bonus, since these speakers don't need to reproduce lower frequencies, the satellite speakers can be quite small and still be totally effective. Figure 4-5 shows just how small the satellite speakers can be, by comparing the size of one of them to the size of a recordable disc jewel case.

Figure 4-5
Satellite speakers can be very small and still produce very good sound.

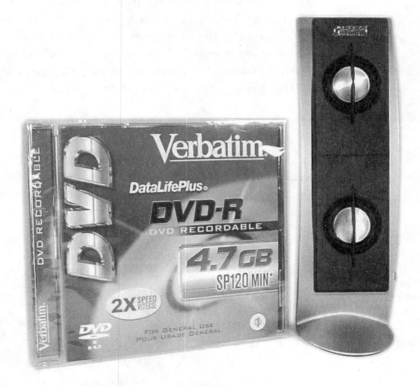

With a solid understanding of how six-speaker systems work, it's easy to see why they're so much more effective than many of the monster speaker systems that were used in the past. By applying the technology, you can simply get far better sound from much smaller packages. Let's take a look at some speaker system options that might be a good match for the home entertainment system PC.

Powered Speaker Systems

Speaker systems that are intended for use with a PC are virtually always powered speaker systems. This means that they have a built-in amplifier. Quite simply, the sound level output from the typical PC sound card just isn't high enough—especially if you want to drive better-quality speakers at higher volume levels.

TIPS OF THE TRADE

Get the Right Speakers

The typical PC speaker system is a stereo system, although many of the better-quality units include a subwoofer to reproduce the sounds that are too low in frequency to be accurately reproduced by the satellite speakers. Even though these systems may be perfectly adequate for typical PC use such as gaming, they probably aren't what you'll want for your home entertainment system PC. Quite simply, you'll want better sound as well as the full Dolby 5.1 surround sound six-channel speaker setup. That way, you'll be able to get the full enjoyment from any DVD movies that you play.

My choice of speakers for the home entertainment system PC project is shown in Figure 4-6. This is the Altec Lansing model 5100 system. As you can see, the speaker system has six enclosures, but it contains 12 speakers since each enclosure has 2 speakers.

Figure 4-6
The Altec Lansing model 5100 speaker system is a perfect match for the home entertainment system PC.

The Altec Lansing model 5100 speaker system also includes a 100-watt amplifier to produce more than adequate sound levels to easily make you very unpopular with your neighbors (and your landlord, if you live in an apartment). I'm especially impressed with certain design features of this system, including the heavyweight metal bases on each of the satellite speakers, and the solid-wood case that houses the woofers and the amplifier. In addition, the gray and black color scheme is a perfect match for the Antec case we're using for this project. Finally, the speaker system has its own remote control so that you can fine-tune the sound to your precise tastes.

Audiophile Speaker Systems

If you're a real audiophile, you probably won't be satisfied with anything less than a top-end speaker system that is connected to a high-quality home theater receiver. If so, you already know that you're going to spend a fair amount of money on your speakers. Still, you'll probably find that the added investment is worth it to you.

To be honest, there are a number of excellent brands in audiophile speaker systems, and choosing one is probably more a matter of personal preference than is the choice of most of the other components of your home entertainment center. It would be very hard to go wrong with almost any of these systems, although some will certainly fit your décor better than others. Listening to the speakers in an audio showroom is probably the best way to make a final decision. However, if you want some places to begin, you might consider the following links. At these sites, you'll find a lot of information that can help you decide on the specific brand and model to suit your needs.

- ❏ Klipsch (www.klipsch.com)
- ❏ Bose (www.bose.com)
- ❏ Denon (www.denon.com)
- ❏ Polk Audio (www.polkaudio.com)

At this point, you should double-check to make certain the following items have been completed:

❑ All the cables inside the case are connected to the correct connectors on the motherboard. The motherboard has small labels by each connector, so if you work carefully you should not have any problems.

❑ The S bracket is installed on the back of the case and its cables are connected to the motherboard.

Chapter 5

Getting the Right
Storage Systems

Tools of the Trade

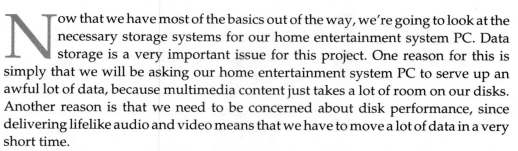

To complete this chapter you'll need:

Maxtor D540X 160GB Ultra ATA/133 hard drive

Generic 3.5-inch floppy disk drive

DVD drive (but you may want to wait with this until Chapter 6)

Spray paint to match the silver and gray Antec case

25-character product key for your copy of Windows XP

Now that we have most of the basics out of the way, we're going to look at the necessary storage systems for our home entertainment system PC. Data storage is a very important issue for this project. One reason for this is simply that we will be asking our home entertainment system PC to serve up an awful lot of data, because multimedia content just takes a lot of room on our disks. Another reason is that we need to be concerned about disk performance, since delivering lifelike audio and video means that we have to move a lot of data in a very short time.

In this chapter, we look at three primary data storage systems. Each of these plays a part in the home entertainment system PC, although not necessarily an equal part. The components we will be choosing in two of the areas—the hard drive and the DVD drive—will be called upon much more heavily than they would in most desktop PCs. Therefore, I will make certain that you understand the issues fully so that you can make the proper choices to get the performance that you want from this system.

Choosing a Hard Drive

It seems almost impossible to believe, but the first PCs didn't include hard drives. In fact, when IBM finally did add the first hard drive to their PCs, it only held 5MB of data. Now, of course, we have digital cameras that have a gigabyte of storage space. Needless to say, the home entertainment system PC will need a pretty large and fast hard disk in order to satisfy all of the demands we will be placing on the system. Let's take a look at some of the considerations we'll be looking at as we choose our hard drive.

A/V Content Burns Space

The first thing that we must consider about a hard drive for the home entertainment system PC is simply that audio/video content uses an awful lot of disk space. The amount of space that is required depends on several factors:

❏ Full-motion video is typically stored at a frame rate of approximately 30 frames per second. To put this in perspective, imagine that for every second of movie or television video that you want to watch, you need to store a high-resolution digital image 30 times. If you have ever used a digital camera, you already know that 30 high-resolution images use a lot of storage space. Now, consider that for each minute of video, you would need 60 times 30, or 1800 individual images. Multiply this times the running time of a typical movie, and you can begin to see why storing full-motion video can take so much room.

❏ In most cases, the multimedia content that we store is actually stored in a compressed format. Typically, for example, we use MPEG compression to reduce the amount of storage that is required. Several different MPEG formats are used for different purposes, and these have a direct effect on the compression ratio and therefore on the amount of disk space that is used.

❏ The larger the size of the video frame—the pixel resolution—the larger the amount of disk space that is required. If you want to capture full-frame video, you will use much more space than if you capture the video at a lower resolution.

❏ Audio typically requires far less disk space than video. You can also use compression on audio data to store the audio in far less space. A well-known example of this is the very popular MP3 format.

TIPS OF THE TRADE

How Much Drive Do You Need?

Although it is not possible to give precise numbers, we can make some estimates of just how much disk space we'll need for the home entertainment system PC. For this, we'll just use some rough numbers. For example, a standard 74-minute audio CD holds approximately 650MB of uncompressed audio. A two-hour DVD movie (which uses MPEG compression) fits on a standard 4.7GB DVD disc. Since we want to be able to record TV shows in real time, as well as use the home entertainment system PC as an on-demand audio jukebox, we're going to need a lot of room. At a minimum, we need at least an 80GB hard drive, although something larger will certainly extend our capabilities.

Disk Performance Equals Playback Quality

Real-time video involves a tremendous amount of streaming data. The system's ability to handle data at a very high rate has a direct effect on the playback quality. If you've ever watched a streaming video presentation on the Web, you've probably noticed that the playback is often rather jerky and seems to pause now and then. The reason for this is quite simple—your PC was not receiving data quickly enough to play the video properly.

On the home entertainment system PC, we want to be able to pause live TV. To do this, the system must be fast enough to be storing new data at the same time that it is displaying existing data. In other words, the PC must enable you to catch up to the show that is being broadcast when you want to resume viewing. But this means that it must be able to show you recorded data at the same time it continues to record. As you can imagine, this can only happen if you have a very fast hard drive.

HEADS UP!

Getting Your Disk Performance for Less

In the past, the only practical way to have a hard drive that was fast enough to keep up with the demands of both recording and playing streaming video was to have a very expensive SCSI hard drive. Recently, however, hard drive manufacturers have been able to produce less-expensive IDE hard drives that have a much higher data transfer rate, allowing those hard drives to be fast enough for multimedia.

ATA/133 Hard Drives

These newer and faster IDE hard drives are designated as ATA/133 hard drives. In this case, the 133 relates to their relative data transfer rate, which is at least double that of ordinary ATA/66 hard drives. ATA/133 hard drives have a theoretical maximum data transfer rate of 133 MB per second. (In reality, data transfer rates are listed as a burst rate, which is much higher than the sustained data transfer rate.) There are also ATA/100 hard drives that fall somewhere in the middle, but they are probably not a much better choice than ATA/66 hard drives for the home entertainment system PC project.

Incidentally, the ATA/133 hard drives are compatible with the older standards, but they will not produce a higher data transfer rate unless they are connected to an ATA/133 controller and unless you are using the proper data cable. The MSI motherboard we have selected for the home entertainment system PC project has built-in ATA/133 controllers, so this will not be a problem for us. Also, the motherboard includes the proper cable.

Watch That Cable

You have to be somewhat careful about your hard drive cables. The older cables and the newer cables are interchangeable, but the newer ones have twice as many wires. Of the 80 wires in the new cables, 40 are ground wires interspersed between the data lines. If you use an old 40-wire cable, the hard drive will still work, but only at the ATA/66 data transfer rate. Clearly, you want to make sure to use the correct cable.

Rotational Speed

In addition to the data transfer rate, hard drives are also rated by rotational speed. Higher rotational speeds result in lower seek times, but this is not as important as the disk capacity and data transfer rate for our purposes. Indeed, the highest-capacity hard disks tend to have lower rotational speeds, but since they have a much higher data density, they are able to seek very quickly since they have far less distance to traverse when the data is packed in more tightly.

Using RAID for Higher Performance

In some cases, even the fastest hard drives just aren't fast enough. One very interesting and innovative way around this is to use something called a *RAID* (redundant array of inexpensive disks). A RAID allows two or more disks to work together in a manner that either greatly improves the overall performance or protects your data through what are essentially automatic backups.

As Figure 5-1 shows, the MSI motherboard includes a Promise RAID controller that you can use to virtually double the throughput of the hard drive system. Note, however, that the Promise RAID controller is an option that may not be on your motherboard.

Figure 5-1
These two connectors
are for the Promise
RAID controller.

Figure 5-1
These two connectors are for the Promise RAID controller.

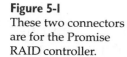

Understanding RAID Configurations

There are several different flavors of RAID configurations. The Promise RAID controller on the MSI motherboard supports RAID 0 and RAID 1. RAID 0 is the performance option, while RAID 1 is the security option. In this case, you would want to configure the controller for RAID 0 (also known as *striping*) in order to achieve the maximum performance.

If you decide to use RAID 0, you need two identical hard drives. Each hard drive must then be connected using an ATA/133 cable to one of the RAID connectors on the motherboard. You can only use two hard drives in your RAID 0 system.

It is possible to use the standard ATA/133 controllers in addition to the RAID controller. Therefore, you don't have to set up your hard drive array at this time unless you want to. You might want to start out with a high-performance ATA/133 hard drive connected to the standard controller, and then add a hard drive array at some later point if you determine that you need additional disk space or higher performance.

The Home Entertainment System PC Hard Drive

After considering the options, I selected the Maxtor D540X 160GB Ultra ATA/133 hard drive, shown in Figure 5-2. This hard drive will provide both the performance and the capacity that we need for the home entertainment system PC.

Figure 5-2
This Maxtor hard drive is an excellent companion to the home entertainment system PC.

The Maxtor D540X 160GB Ultra ATA/133 hard drive has enough capacity that we will be able to record many hours of video as well as hundreds of hours of audio without running short of space. It comes with Maxtor's MaxBlast Plus II software, which will help you properly configure the hard drive. We'll look at the installation and configuration of this hard drive later in this chapter. For now, though, let's move to the next piece of our storage puzzle—a floppy disk drive.

Adding a Floppy Disk Drive

Frankly, when I first started planning the home entertainment system PC, I had no intention of including a floppy disk drive. I figured that a floppy disk drive would be of little use in this PC, especially since disks hold far too little data to be of any value for a multimedia transfer media. Besides, when was the last time you really used disks for data storage, anyway?

Unfortunately, I soon discovered a reality I hadn't counted upon. Even though most PC users seldom store anything on disks, there are still some device manufacturers who distribute device drivers on disk. If you don't have a floppy disk drive, you can't install the drivers and can't use your device. Therefore, a floppy disk drive may still be necessary to enable you to complete your home entertainment system PC.

Choosing a Floppy Disk Drive

Choosing a floppy disk drive was probably one of the easier selections I had to make for this project. Since this is a drive that will seldom be used, the primary consideration in choosing the drive is cost. I picked up a generic 3.5-inch drive for just under $20. There's really no need to spend more on this item.

Painting the Floppy Disk Drive

When you open the box that contains the floppy disk drive, one of your first thoughts will almost certainly be about how ugly that beige drive is going to look in your beautiful silver and gray Antec case (or whatever color you ended up getting). Well, that's part of the idea behind buying a cheap, generic floppy disk drive—you won't feel bad about painting it to match the case. In fact, you might even consider this to be a practice run for a bit later in this chapter when you install a DVD drive. Once you've painted the bezel on the front of the floppy disk drive, you'll feel a lot more confident about painting the front of the DVD drive.

Paint, of course, is not a particularly good thing to get all over the insides of a floppy disk drive (nor a DVD drive, for that matter). If you want the drive to work once the paint is dry, you're going to have to exercise a certain amount of care to keep the paint out of the insides.

Let's take a look at how you can paint the bezel and not cause any damage:

1. Take the drive out of the box. Figure 5-3 shows the drive before I started removing the bezel.

Figure 5-3
The floppy disk
drive before painting
the bezel

2. Remove the protective cover on the bottom of the drive. In most cases,
    you simply need to use a small screwdriver to gently pry out the cover
    past the tabs, as shown in Figure 5-4. You may need to remove screws
    on some drives. Don't touch any of the components under the cover
    while it is off.

Figure 5-4
Carefully pry off
the bottom cover.

3. In most cases, you can remove the bezel by gently lifting the tabs holding it to the case, as shown in Figure 5-5. Be very careful here so that you do not break any of the tabs. Work a little from each side until the bezel comes off.

Figure 5-5
Remove the bezel
by gently lifting
these tabs.

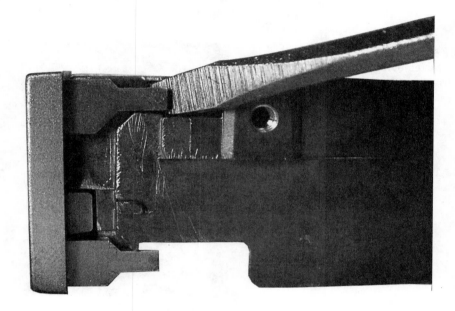

4. When the bezel has been removed, cover the LED lens with a small piece of tape. Take your time to make sure you are as neat as possible, since any errors you make here will be visible after you've painted the bezel.

5. Using spray paint that matches the front panel of the case, spray the bezel with several very light coats of paint. Make certain that the bezel is sitting on a flat surface and that each coat is hardly more than a dusting—otherwise, the paint may run or sag. It's much better to be very patient so that the end result is attractive than to be in a hurry and create a mess. When the paint is dry, you can reinstall the bezel onto the drive.

If you don't like the look of the beige disk eject button, I'd suggest spraying some paint into a small container (like a paper cup) and using a small brush to paint the button. That way, you won't be spraying paint into the drive. Remember to allow plenty of time for the paint to dry before you handle any of the pieces.

Installing the Floppy Disk Drive

Once the paint is completely dry, you can install the floppy disk drive. Let's go through the procedure step by step to make things as clear and easy as possible.

1. Press the release tabs on each side of the upper-front cover on the case, as shown in Figure 5-6. This will enable you to pull the cover forward and off.

Figure 5-6
Begin by removing the drive cover.

2. When you have removed the cover, carefully press the tabs that hold the bottom drive plate in place, as shown in Figure 5-7. You need to press the tabs on both sides so that the drive plate can slide out the front. Set the cover aside after you have removed the drive plate.

Figure 5-7
Remove the drive plate so there is an opening for the floppy disk drive.

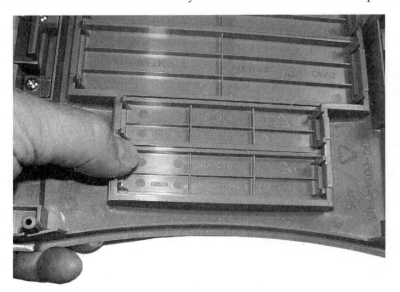

3. Unscrew the thumbscrews at each side of the floppy disk drive cage and slide the cage out the front of the case, as shown in Figure 5-8. You need to remove the cage so that you can fasten the drive into the cage.

Figure 5-8
Slide the drive cage out so you can install the drive.

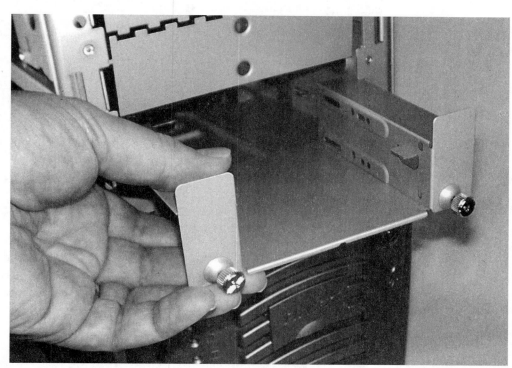

4. Slide the drive into the lower position in the drive cage and then fasten it in place using four of the fine-threaded bolts from the hardware kit provided with the drive, as shown in Figure 5-9. Make certain that you choose the correct bolts—if they seem to bind, you have the wrong ones. You may have to experiment to find the correct position for the drive, so don't tighten the screws until the alignment is correct. The front of the drive should line up with the front of the drive plates, and this may be further forward than you expect. I recommend testing the fit before you connect any cables.

Figure 5-9
Fasten the drive
into the cage.

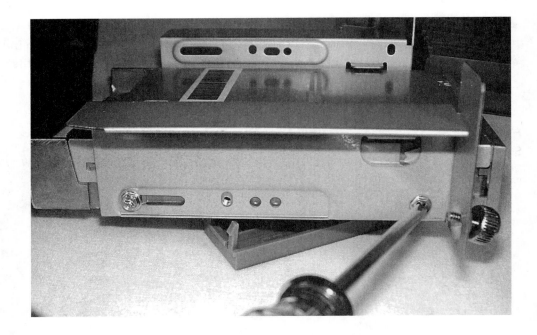

5.   Locate the floppy drive cable and determine where the key is on the
     end connector, as shown in Figure 5-10. Notice that this is the connector
     at the end of the cable where a portion of the cable is twisted. You
     should also note that one edge of the cable has a colored wire that
     corresponds to pin 1 on the floppy disk drive.

Figure 5-10
The drive cable has a
key on the middle of
the bottom edge.

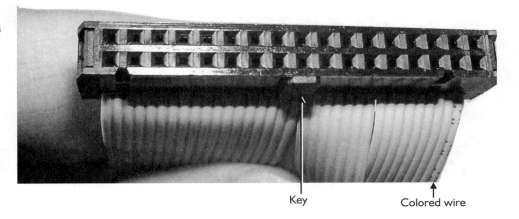

Key   Colored wire

6.   Take a look at the socket on the back of the drive to determine how the
     keyed connector on the drive cable fits into it, as shown in Figure 5-11.
     Then, carefully plug the cable into the drive.

Figure 5-11
The socket on the drive has a notch where the key on the drive cable fits.

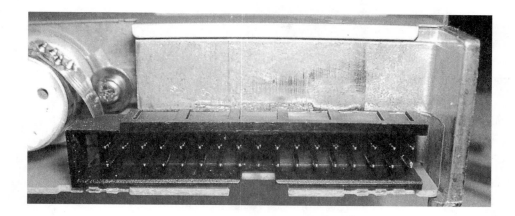

7. Slide the drive cage into the case and tighten the thumbscrews. You need to be careful with the drive cable so that it does not snag on anything as you're sliding the cage in.

8. Once you've determined the best routing for the cable, take two small nylon ties and carefully bundle the cable, as shown in Figure 5-12. You should be able to create a flat bundle by using a small tie on each side.

Figure 5-12
Keep things neat by bundling the cable.

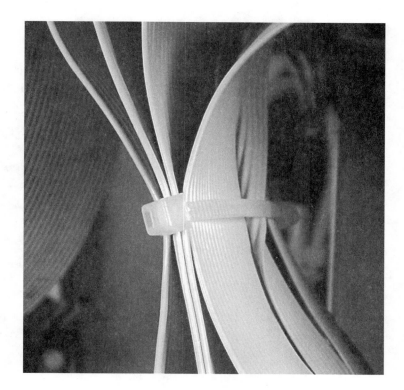

9. Plug the drive cable into the black FDD1 connector on the motherboard, as shown in Figure 5-13. This end of the cable is also keyed so that it can only be inserted in the correct direction.

Figure 5-13
Connect the drive cable to the motherboard.

10. Find one of the small power connectors and plug it into the floppy disk drive, as shown in Figure 5-14. Note that this connector has a ridge along one side that should stick up as you slide the connector into place. This ridge also prevents you from installing the plug upside down.

Figure 5-14
Plug in the power connector to the drive.

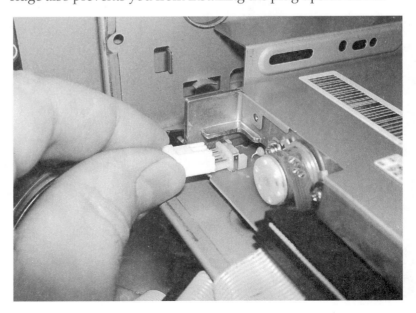

11. Snap the front cover onto the case. Figure 5-15 shows how the drive should look once it has been installed.

Figure 5-I5
The floppy disk drive is now fully installed and ready to use.

Choosing a DVD Drive

The next type of storage we'll be adding is a DVD drive. DVDs are the same physical size as an audio CD, but they are recorded in a different format that gives them many times more storage space. Fortunately, DVD drives are quite capable of reading audio CDs. This means that a single drive can serve dual purposes.

Playing Movies

These days, most movies are distributed on DVDs rather than on VHS videotape. There are a number of reasons for this, not the least of which is that DVDs are less expensive to produce, more durable, and less prone to easy copying.

We'll be using a DVD drive in the home entertainment system PC to make it possible to play DVD movies. Keep in mind that you will also need software that enables the home entertainment system PC to play DVD movies. In most cases, this software is included with the DVD drive.

Playing Audio CDs

Because DVD drives can also read audio CDs, you will be able to not only play audio CDs, but also copy your favorite music from audio CDs onto the home entertainment system PC hard drive.

Considering a Combo Drive

Many DVD drives are known as combo drives. Generally, this means that they also are able to record onto CD-R and CD-RW discs. As you will see in the next chapter, I have gone a step up from the combo drives for the home entertainment system PC, by choosing a DVD-RW drive. This type of drive has all the capabilities of the combo drives as well as the ability to write to DVD-R and DVD-RW discs.

Painting the DVD Drive

The DVD drive presents a slight dilemma for the home entertainment system PC builder. Although painting the face of the drive to match the computer case would certainly improve the overall appearance of the finished project, painting a DVD drive is a lot more difficult than painting the floppy disk drive. One reason for this is that the bezel on the front of the DVD drive is not easily removable, making it much more difficult to paint the drive without risking damage to it. In addition, the DVD drive has a number of openings on the front that just seem to beg paint to enter. As you can imagine, getting paint inside the DVD drive would wreak havoc on it.

Ultimately, the choice of whether or not you paint the DVD drive is yours. One option you might want to consider is to trim a large stick-on label to fit the front of the drive, and then to paint the label before you apply it. Although I agree this would be a lot of work, it certainly lessens the chance that you will damage the drive by painting it. Another option you might want to try is to very carefully paint the front of the drive using a small brush. Personally, I will probably live with the standard front on the DVD drive—although I may change my mind and paint it at some point in the future.

Installing the DVD Drive

Okay, so let's install the DVD drive. This process is similar to installing the floppy disk drive, with a few minor differences. Here's what you need to do:

1. If you have reinstalled the drive cover on the front of the case, remove it now by pressing in the two tabs and pulling forward (refer back to Figure 5-6).

2. Remove the metal cover plate from the top drive bay by bending it, as shown in Figure 5-16. You may have to bend it back and forth several times to break it free.

Figure 5-16
Only remove the metal plate for the drive bay you intend to use.

3. Take two of the drive rails from the storage area at the bottom of the case and mount one on each side of the DVD drive, as shown in Figure 5-17. Be sure to use the proper screws from the hardware kit provided with the drive so that you do not damage the drive.

Figure 5-17
Fasten a drive rail on each side of the DVD drive.

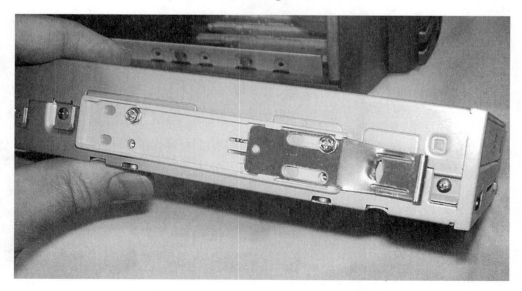

4. Make certain that the jumper is set to the master position, as shown in Figure 5-18. The jumpers are located on the back of the drive—in this case, they are just below the small cooling fan.

Figure 5-18
Set the drive jumper to master.

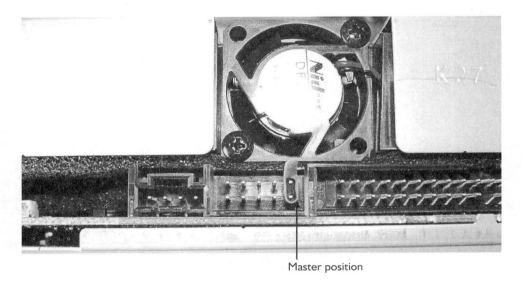

Master position

5. Plug the black connector of the ribbon cable into the drive. as shown in Figure 5-19. The connector is keyed so that it will only fit into the socket in the correct direction.

Figure 5-19
Make sure the black plug on the ribbon cable is fully seated.

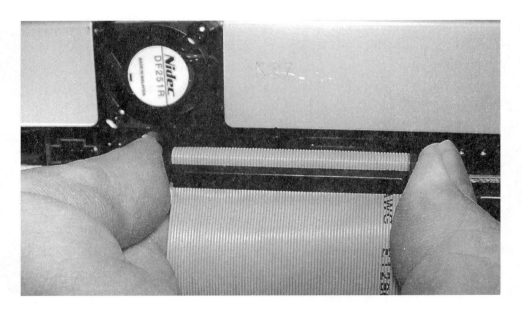

6. Plug the audio cable into the socket, as shown in Figure 5-20. If your DVD drive does not include the audio cable, buy a standard CD-ROM to sound card audio cable at your local parts outlet. Note, however, that there is no reason to pay the $25 asking price at some big name stores when you can buy the same cable for $5 from an electronic supplies shop.

Figure 5-20
Attach the
audio cable.

7. Slide the drive into the case, as shown in Figure 5-21. It will snap into place when it is fully seated. Be careful with the cables as you slide the drive in.

Figure 5-21
The drive should slide
easily into the mount.

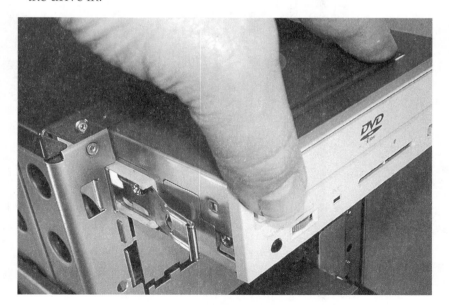

8. Plug the audio cable into the JCD socket on the motherboard. I've found that if I route the audio cable behind the motherboard, it will easily fit the distance between the JCD socket and the DVD drive, and this positioning offers the side benefit of keeping the cable out of the way.

9. Plug the blue connector on the ribbon cable into the IDE2 socket on the motherboard, as shown in Figure 5-22. Once again, the connector and the socket are keyed to make sure you install the cable correctly.

Figure 5-22
Make certain you plug the cable into the IDE2 socket.

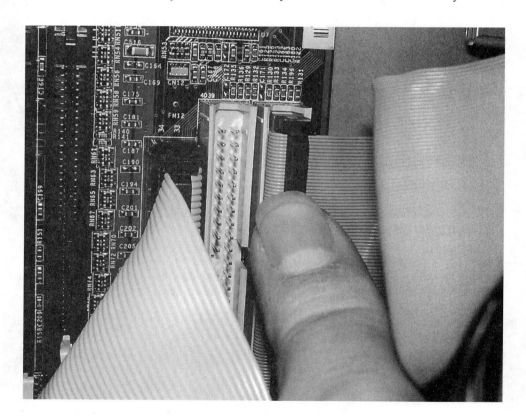

10. If you will not be installing another device on this ribbon cable, carefully bundle the cable with two ties (as you did with the floppy disk drive cable).

11. Plug one of the large power connectors into the back of the drive. These connectors are shaped to prevent you from inserting them incorrectly.

If you are installing a second DVD drive, follow the same procedure, except for setting the jumper on the back of the drive. The second DVD drive should be configured as the slave. This drive will then be connected to the gray connector on the ribbon cable.

Installing the Hard Drive

We've now come down to the final important piece of hardware that makes up our basic home entertainment system PC. Installing the hard drive involves several tasks unlike those we've encountered so far. We, do, of course, have to physically install the hard drive in a manner similar to the way we installed the floppy disk drive and the DVD drive, but we also must begin with some of the software installation, too.

Specifically, we'll need to partition and then format the drive, and once those tasks are complete, we'll need to install the operating system. Once all of this has been completed, we'll have a functioning computer for the first time in the project. At that point, we'll be in a position to begin installing the software that will make the system into our home entertainment system PC.

Different Procedures May Apply in Your Case

Please keep in mind that if you've selected a different hard drive than the Maxtor D540X 160GB Ultra ATA/133 I've chosen for this project, you may have some different steps in partitioning and formatting your hard drive. Unfortunately, I can't really anticipate what you'll encounter—especially if you're using a different brand of hard drive. You should be able to figure out what you need to do by following along with the text, however, since ultimately you'll be completing quite similar tasks in any case. When in doubt, RTM (Read the Manual).

Mounting and Connecting the Hard Drive

Since mounting the hard drive is so similar to the steps we've followed mounting the other two drives, we'll step through this procedure fairly quickly. Here's what you need to do:

1. Check the jumpers on the back of the hard drive, as shown in Figure 5-23. Make certain that the drive is set as the master.

Figure 5-23
Set the jumpers to master.

2. Plug the black connector of the ATA/133 ribbon cable into the drive, as shown in Figure 5-24. Make certain that the key on the connector lines up with the notch on the socket.

Figure 5-24
Use the black connector at the end of the ATA/133 cable.

3. Slide the drive cage out by first pulling the lever back and then moving the cage back (see Figure 5-25). Be careful so that you do not snag any of the cables.

Figure 5-25
Pull the drive cage out so you can mount the hard drive.

4. Mount the hard drive using four bolts (included with the drive). Note that the hard drive will stick out the back of the drive cage.

5. Slide the drive cage back into the case and push the lever forward to latch it.

6. Plug the blue connector on the ribbon cable into the IDE1 socket on the motherboard. You should always avoid placing hard drives and DVD (or CD-ROM) drives on the same IDE controller, to reduce the possibility of problems.

7. Plug one of the large power connectors into the drive, as shown in Figure 5-26.

Figure 5-26
Plug in the power connector to complete the physical installation.

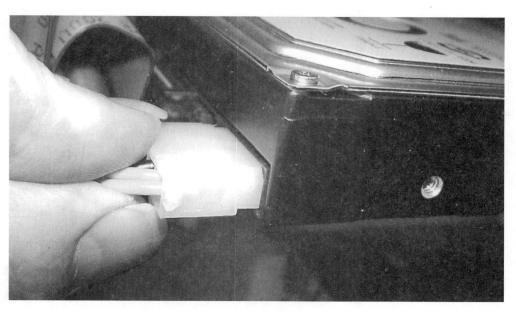

Partitioning and Formatting the Hard Drive

Now it's time to prepare the hard drive electronically. To do this, you will need to connect a keyboard, a mouse, a monitor, and the power cord to the home entertainment system PC. Once you have done so, you'll have the thrill of seeing your system come alive for the first time.

Before we continue, I'd like to mention that the remaining figures in this chapter are photographs of the computer screen, and therefore may not be quite as clear as a normal screen capture. Unfortunately, the tasks of partitioning and formatting the hard drive as well as installing Windows XP must be done using special-purpose operating environments that are not conducive to the use of our normal screen-capture software. I hope you'll understand that we've done the best we can to give you the clearest picture possible of these procedures.

Here are the steps you'll need to follow to prepare your hard drive for use in the home entertainment system PC:

1. Connect a keyboard, mouse, and monitor to your home entertainment system PC. These do not have to be the components you will use once the system is fully set up. For example, if you're eventually going to use a cordless keyboard and mouse, you'll need to borrow standard wired ones to use for now.

2. Plug in the power cord and turn on the power. You need to first turn on the power switch on the back of the power supply and then press the power button on the front of the case.

3. When the system begins displaying messages on the screen, watch to see if it has identified the hard drive. As long as the correct brand of hard drive is shown, you won't need to enter the BIOS setup, since this means that the hard drive was recognized properly. If the system does not start up or does not recognize the hard drive, turn off the power and check to make certain that all of the cables are fully seated and that the processor is correctly installed.

4. Place the MaxBlast disk and CD-ROM into the drives when you see the message telling you to insert a bootable disk, and then press a key to continue.

5. When you see the MaxBlast menu, select MaxBlast Plus II to display the welcome screen. Click Next to continue.

6. When you are given the option to choose a drive, as shown in Figure 5-27, choose the Maxtor hard drive and click Next to continue.

Figure 5-27
Partition and format the hard drive.

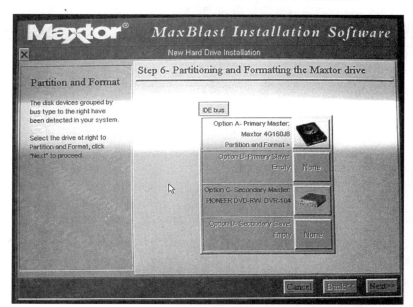

7. When you see the screen titled, "No Operating System Detected," click the Choose OS button. This will enable you to select Windows XP, which does not offer the option to boot from disks. (Note that if you attempt to create bootable disks from within Windows XP, the disk will actually contain the operating system files for Windows Me rather than Windows XP.)

8. In the next screen that appears, click the Windows XP option, as shown in Figure 5-28.

Figure 5-28
Choose Windows XP.

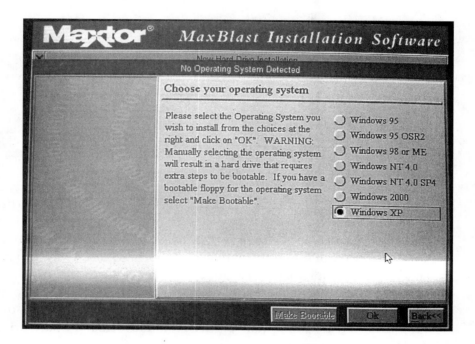

9. Click the OK button to continue.

10. When you see the screen asking you to choose a partition method, choose the partitioning option you prefer. Unless you want to split the drive into more than one partition, you can choose the Standard Partitions option.

11. Click Next to continue.

12. Finally, when you see the screen shown in Figure 5-29, click the Finish button to complete the partitioning and formatting process. Along the way, you may see some warnings about this being your last chance to change your mind. If so, confirm that you want to continue.

Figure 5-29
The partition is about
to be created.

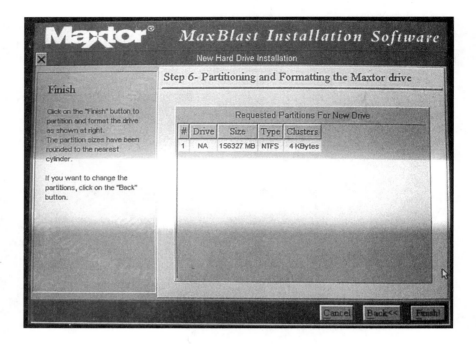

If you encounter error messages during the partitioning and formatting process, you may need to start over and carefully check the options you select. In some cases, it may even be necessary to get a little creative in trying out different options. Unfortunately, it's very hard to predict which combinations of BIOS versions and software versions may cause some problems. The best advice I can offer if you do have a problem is to keep on trying—sooner or later you will come across a combination that works for you. Remember, the goal here is simply to create one or more partitions and to format the hard drive so that you can install the operating system.

Installing the Operating System

Once the hard drive has been partitioned and formatted, it's time to take the next step that will turn the home entertainment system PC into a real, usable computer system—installing the operating system. In this case, we'll be installing Windows XP.

Installing Windows XP is a pretty simple process since everything is quite straightforward and easy to understand. Primarily, it's a matter of answering a few questions and waiting while the mostly automated procedure moves forward. Because of this, I'm not going to bore you by covering each individual step along the way. Rather, I'll mention some of the important things you'll see and let you mostly just respond to the prompts you'll see on the screen.

So, let's install Windows XP on the home entertainment system PC:

1. Place the Windows XP disc into the DVD drive and then restart the system. You can do this by pressing the Reset button or by powering down and then back up.

2. When you see the Welcome to Setup screen, press ENTER to begin the setup process. This will begin copying files and will take several minutes.

3. Eventually the system will restart in a graphical mode (see Figure 5-30) and begin working to install Windows XP. You'll need to enter your name before you can click Next to continue.

Figure 5-30
Most of the Windows XP installation will be automated, but you will have to answer a few questions.

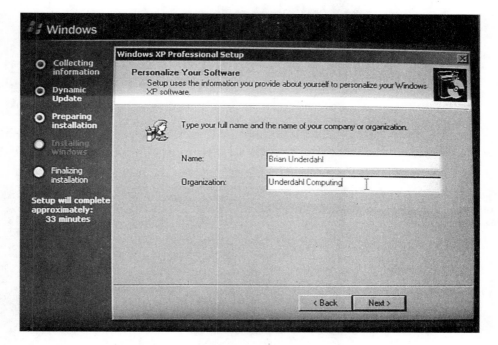

4. When you see the screen shown in Figure 5-31, you will have to enter the 25-character product key for your copy of Windows XP. Each product key can only be used one time, and you must enter it exactly as shown on the sticker for it to be accepted. After you have entered your product key, click Next to continue.

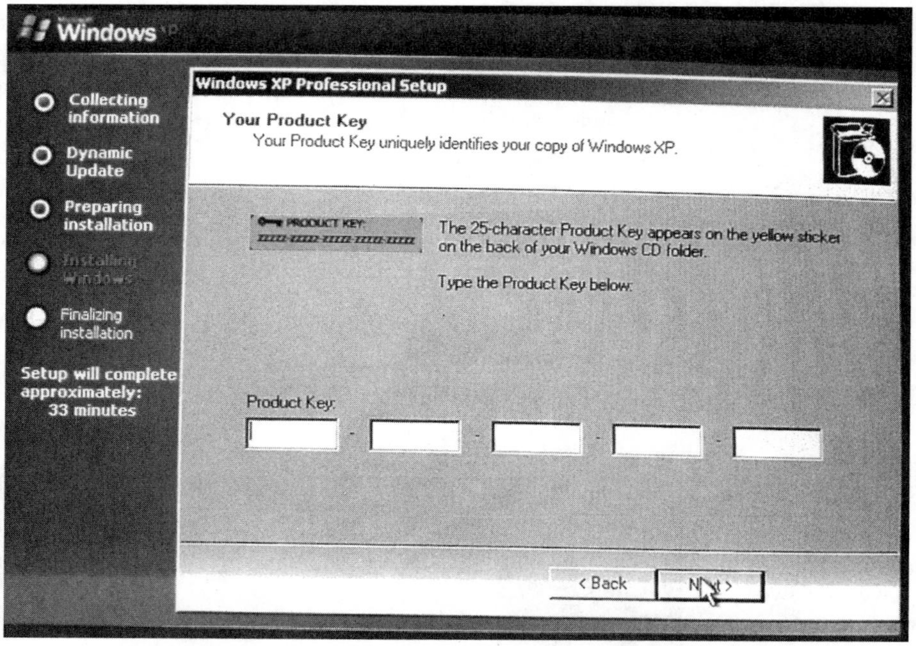

Figure 5-31
You must enter
a valid, unused
product key to
install Windows XP.

5. Eventually you will see the screen shown in Figure 5-32. Enter your
    name and click Next.

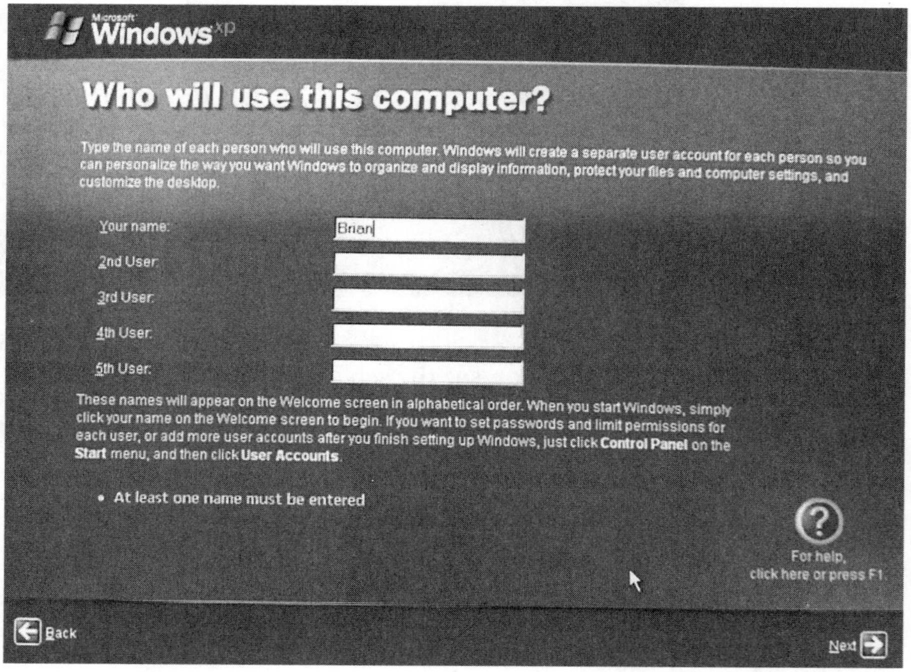

Figure 5-32
You must enter at
least one name.

During the installation process, you will be given the opportunity to activate your copy of Windows XP. It is best to decline for now since you will still be making some changes to your home entertainment system PC, and these changes can result in requiring you to reactivate the OS. It's best to wait until you have finalized the system configuration before activating Windows XP, since reactivating it can be a somewhat frustrating and time-consuming process. You have 30 days before you must activate Windows XP.

At this point, your home entertainment system PC will be running, but it won't be optimized. You'll probably notice one deficiency right away—your screen may not look quite as good as you expect. The reason for this is simply that you still need to install the correct drivers for the various system components, such as the display adapter. Once you do, you'll find that your home entertainment system PC will function far better than it does now.

In addition to lacking the correct drivers, your home entertainment system PC is also lacking some very important application software. In Chapter 9, we'll take a look at both the necessary drivers and the software you'll need to make everything work together to do what you want. In the next few chapters, though, we'll look at some additional hardware options you'll want to consider first.

**TESTING
1-2-3**

At this point, you should double-check to make certain the following items have been completed:

❏ If you painted the floppy disk drive and the DVD drive to match the case, make certain that you gave the paint plenty of time to dry before handling the drives.

❏ The hard drive, the floppy disk drive, and the DVD drive have been installed into the case. You will need to connect the data cable and the power cable for each drive.

❏ The hard drive has been successfully partitioned and formatted.

❏ Windows XP has been installed. You will need to enter your product key during the installation, and you will need to activate Windows XP within 30 days. Remember, each product key can only be used on one computer.

Distributing
Your Content

Tools of the Trade

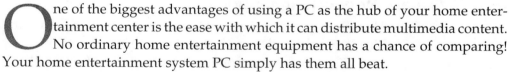

To complete this chapter you'll need:
Pioneer DVR-104 DVD-R/RW drive
Network adapter card
Ethernet cables—a crossover cable if you're just connecting two PCs,
or patch cables if you're connecting more than two PCs
A hub, switch, or router if you're connecting more than two PCs
Optional—the Bluetooth kit for use with the MSI motherboard
Optional—SnapStream PVS if you want to distribute streaming video on your network

One of the biggest advantages of using a PC as the hub of your home entertainment center is the ease with which it can distribute multimedia content. No ordinary home entertainment equipment has a chance of comparing! Your home entertainment system PC simply has them all beat.

There are several different ways to distribute the content generated on your home entertainment system PC. In this chapter, we'll have a look at burning CDs and DVDs that can then be played on another PC, in a stand-alone DVD player, or (in the case of audio CDs) even in your car. We'll also look at some options for distributing content to other PCs in your home through a network. This will enable you to use any PC you own to view TV shows or listen to music even if your home entertainment system PC is being used for some other purpose. Finally, we'll look at how you can wirelessly send both audio and video signals from your home entertainment system PC to TV sets, stereo receivers, or even powered speakers throughout your home with the use of another PC.

Networking Your Content

If you have more than one PC, sharing data between your different systems is quite often a very convenient way to make better use of those computers. Since multimedia content is really just a form of data, it makes a lot of sense for you to share the content from your home entertainment system PC with any other PCs you might have in your home. (Frankly, I'd be somewhat surprised if you'd be even thinking about building your home entertainment system PC if you weren't already a computer user.)

TIPS OF
THE TRADE

Throughput Reigns

There are quite a few different networking options for PCs, but they all serve a similar purpose—allowing two or more computers to easily share information. But even though they can accomplish the same tasks, those networking options vary considerably in throughput (the speed at which data can be shared), ease of installation, operating distance, and overall cost. Of these factors, throughput is by far the dominate item you must consider if you want to be able to *stream* multimedia content over your network (I'll discuss content streaming a bit later in this chapter). As you will soon see, however, there is a very definite interaction between all of the primary selection factors, so you may need to compromise in certain areas to gain in others.

Wireless Networking Options

There's no question that wireless networking holds quite an appeal. The whole idea is simply cool—you just pop in a wireless network adapter and suddenly your PCs can communicate without a bunch of wires. What could be easier?

Unfortunately, the realities of wireless networking fall somewhat short of the expectations. Let's take a look at each of the three main wireless networking options in use today so that you can see what I mean.

802.11b—WiFi

The most common form of wireless networking is what is known as *802.11b*, also called WiFi. This type of wireless networking, like all wireless networks, uses small radio transceivers to send and receive data. WiFi operates in the 2.4 GHz radio band, on an unlicensed group of frequencies that is shared by such things as cordless phones, microwave ovens, and Bluetooth devices.

Figure 6-1 shows a typical WiFi *access point* (this one happens to be made by Proxim—www.proxim.com). An access point is a transceiver that connects devices to your network by radio.

Figure 6-1
This is the Proxim
WiFi Access Point
connected to my
network.

Although you do not need to run a whole bunch of cables to install an 802.11b wireless network, there are some other things that argue against using this type of network to distribute multimedia content from your home entertainment system PC:

❏ Although the theoretical maximum data speed of an 802.11b network is 11 Mbps (megabits per second), the speed drops off with distance from the access point. In addition, interference from other devices using the 2.4 GHz band tends to reduce the throughput. My personal experience has shown typical speeds closer to 1 Mbps, which is simply too slow for good streaming video performance.

❏ The access point is required, and at a few hundred dollars each, the costs add up quickly. This is in addition to the wireless adapter you'll need for each PC (and these aren't cheap, either).

Wireless Security Considerations

Most WiFi networks are wide-open doors in terms of security. The security features are typically turned off by default, and configuring them can be a nightmare. You might not think of this as a problem until you realize that inadequate security could allow a stranger easy access to your entire network from hundreds of feet away. This would make it possible to snoop through your files, steal sensitive information, or even plant computer viruses.

802.11a

802.11a wireless networking is similar to WiFi in many respects, but it uses a different frequency band and is incompatible with WiFi. The typical throughput for 802.11a wireless networks is much higher than for WiFi networks, but this doesn't make 802.11a a perfect choice, either. Consider these shortcomings:

❏ 802.11a wireless networks also require access points and although they look very similar to access points for 802.11b, 802.11a access points cost quite a bit more than 802.11b access points. Typically, they may be as much as twice as expensive.

❏ The wireless 802.11a adapters are also more expensive than their 802.11b counterparts.

❏ Security for 802.11a wireless networks is only slightly improved by the higher-frequency band where they operate, but that small improvement is probably more than offset by the longer range of 802.11a. In other words, with an 802.11a wireless network, an intruder could operate from an even greater distance from your home than if you had a WiFi network.

Bluetooth

Bluetooth is a fairly low-power wireless option that works in the same 2.4 GHz band as WiFi. It is not, however, compatible with WiFi, and the two can easily interfere with each other.

Bluetooth vs. Multimedia Content

Bluetooth is really not a viable option for distributing multimedia content. At its fastest, it is less than half the slowest WiFi speed. In addition, Bluetooth devices have a very limited range—often less than 30 feet.

Even though Bluetooth is not really a viable option for distributing multimedia content from your home entertainment system PC, you should be aware that MSI—the manufacturer of our home entertainment system PC motherboard—offers a Bluetooth kit for use with this motherboard (see Figure 6-2).

Figure 6-2
This kit adds
Bluetooth capability
to the home
entertainment
system PC.

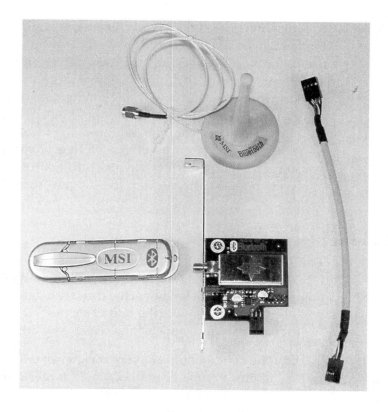

Why should this interest you? Well, Bluetooth is useful for a number of purposes:

❏ If you have a Pocket PC, Bluetooth is a low-power method of enabling your Pocket PC and your home entertainment system PC to communicate. Power consumption is always an important factor when you're dealing with a Pocket PC.

❏ Some notebook computers have Bluetooth transceivers built in. This can provide a convenient way for a notebook user to connect to your network without the necessity of plugging into a network cable.

❏ Some printers offer a Bluetooth option, which means that you can place the printer anywhere within range and print without running a printer cable.

Wireless Networking for Your Entertainment PC?

There's no getting around the fact that wireless networking can be pretty cool. In fact, I have a wireless WiFi network in my home office in addition to a wired network. The WiFi network enables me to take a laptop PC or a Pocket PC wherever I want to in the office and still be able to access my network.

I also have several pieces of Bluetooth equipment in my office. The more-limited range and lower speed means that the Bluetooth connection isn't nearly as useful for most networking purposes, but it's still handy for some things.

Ultimately, though, I'm not going to be using any type of wireless networking to connect the home entertainment system PC to my other PCs. When I want to supply streaming video to those other PCs, when I want to swap large files, or when I have confidential files I don't want some neighbor being able to access wirelessly, I simply feel that wireless won't really do the job at this point. You may find that a wireless network fulfills all of your networking needs, but be ready for higher costs, slower speeds, and reduced security as a part of the bargain.

Ethernet Networking

The old standard of PC networking—Ethernet—is still the most popular. In an Ethernet network, each PC is connected to a small cable that runs to a central point (or two PCs can be connected directly together without that central point if you only want to connect the two of them).

The following are some of the reasons why Ethernet networks are so popular:

❑ The components are very inexpensive. It's not uncommon to be able to buy a name-brand network adapter card (like the Linksys unit shown in Figure 6-3) for around $10. Likewise, cables and hubs are also quite inexpensive.

Figure 6-3
Inexpensive Ethernet adapters are very easy to find.

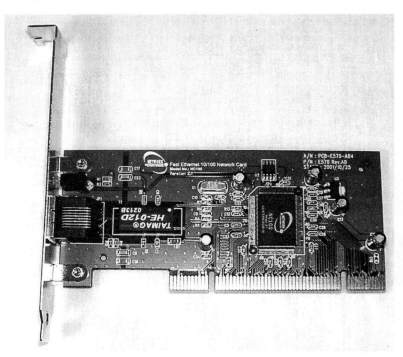

❏ Ethernet networks offer the highest speeds of any PC networks. Most PC Ethernet networks now operate at 100 Mbps, while 1000 Mbps is also starting to appear. In other words, Ethernet networks typically offer throughput up to 100 times faster than the norm for wireless networks.

❏ Security on Ethernet networks is relatively easy to configure. In fact, the Windows XP operating system we've selected for this project automatically applies security locks to all resources, and warns you if you attempt to reduce the security settings. In addition, an intruder would need physical access to your network to do any damage (unless you ignore the warnings and open your network connection to the Internet, of course).

❏ Ethernet networks are also fairly easy to set up. You can buy all the components ready to go, or you can pick and choose just what you need. If necessary, you can even wire your own cables if you need to handle a tricky wiring situation.

Networking Two PCs

Ethernet networks can be used to connect two or more PCs. Although that may sound obvious, it's also the source of some slight confusion for first-time network builders. The reason for this confusion is that there are two different types of cables you can use on a typical Ethernet network, and while the two look identical externally, they are electrically incompatible.

When you have more than two PCs connected to the network, every PC connects to a central point (which I'll discuss shortly) using the standard type of Ethernet cable—a *patch* cable. But if you only have two PCs, it is possible to connect the two together directly using a *crossover* cable. Unfortunately, a patch cable and a crossover cable look exactly alike, and the only indication of the difference between the two is that using the wrong one will prevent your network from functioning. You won't, however, receive an error message telling you that you have the wrong type of cable—your network simply won't work.

Crossover Cable Confusion

The best advice I can offer regarding crossover cables is this: you never need more than one crossover cable no matter how large your network becomes, and it should be clearly labeled so that it is never confused with a patch cable. Add your own label at each end of the crossover cable. You may even want to buy a crossover cable in an odd color as a reminder that it is different from your other cables. Also, if you intend to use a hub, switch, or router as the center point of your network, you probably don't even need a single crossover cable.

Hubs, Switches, and Routers

If you want to network three or more PCs, you need a device that serves to collect the network signals at a central point and then distribute those signals around the network. This device can be a *hub*, *switch*, or *router*. For a very small network (such as one you might have in your home), there isn't a whole lot of difference between the three. Generally speaking, a hub is the least expensive, a switch is somewhat more expensive, and a router is the most expensive. In addition, both performance and complexity increase somewhat as you move from a hub to a switch, or from a switch to a router.

The most important factor for a small home network is making certain that the hub, switch, or router that you buy has enough ports. You need one port for each PC on your network. I generally recommend buying a unit that has a couple of spare ports so that you'll have room for future expansion.

I've found the Linksys (www.linksys.com) networking hardware to be an excellent choice. The Linksys EZXS16W 16-port switch, shown in Figure 6-4, may be more than you need, but then you probably don't have as many computers in your home office as I do. You'll find network hubs and switches with as few as five ports at the Linksys web site.

Figure 6-4
This Linksys switch provides excellent network throughput.

Although it's less common today than a few years ago, you'll also want to make certain that the unit you buy is compatible with *100BaseT* and not just *10BaseT*. A 100BaseT network can operate at 100 Mbps, compared to 10 Mbps for 10BaseT. Most hubs, switches, and routers are compatible with both standards, but you should watch for this to make certain you aren't getting stuck with the older, slower models.

Cat 5 Cabling

Ethernet networks use *Cat 5* cables. These are cables similar to telephone wire, and they even use plugs that look like large telephone plugs (Cat 5 cable plugs are RJ-45 plugs rather than the slightly smaller RJ-11 plugs used on telephone cords, however).

Cat 5 cables contain eight wires arranged as four twisted pairs. Each pair has one wire that is mostly one color and another wire that has some of that color but is mostly white. The four pairs are blue, orange, green, and brown.

Most people buy premade Cat 5 cables, but you can assemble your own cables from Cat 5 wire and RJ-45 connectors. Figure 6-5 shows how the larger Cat 5 cable and RJ-45 connector compare to the smaller telephone cable with an RJ-11 connector.

Figure 6-5
Cat 5 network cables are larger than ordinary telephone wiring.

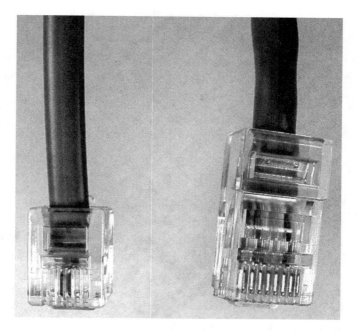

You'll probably need to buy a crimping tool to properly seat the connectors. Figure 6-6 shows the Ideal 30-496 tool I use. It might be possible to use pliers to seat the connectors, but it's hard to say what kind of results you would get (and remember that a poor connection could easily prevent your network from working correctly).

Figure 6-6
This crimping tool makes assembling network cables much easier.

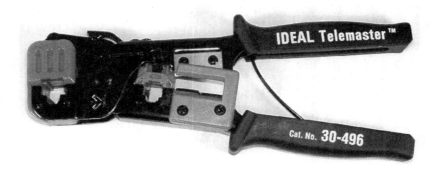

If you decide that you need to make your own network cables—perhaps because you need to be able to run the wire through a wall—start by buying the Cat 5 wire, the RJ-45 connectors, and the crimping tool. Then follow these steps:

1. Strip about 1 inch from the end of the wire jacket.

2. Fan out the wires so that each white member of a pair is next to the colored member of the pair. The white wire should be to the left of the colored wire, and the pairs should be in this order: blue, orange, green, and brown.

3. Hold the wires together so that they are still in the same order and then trim the end of the bundle straight across so that the wires are 1/2 inch beyond the jacket.

4. Carefully slide the wires into the RJ-45 plug (with the pins up on the connector) until they are fully seated.

5. Use the crimping tool to crimp the connector and fasten the wires solidly in place.

If you are creating a patch cable to connect a PC to a hub, switch, or router, repeat the same process for the other end of the cable. If you are creating a crossover cable, modify the layout of the wires so that the orange and green pairs are swapped at the second end of the cable. That is, the second end of a crossover cable should have the wire pairs in this order: blue, green, orange, and brown. The white wire from each pair must still be on the left.

Hiding Your Ethernet Cabling

The biggest objection that people seem to have to Ethernet networks as compared to wireless networks is that you have to run those cables all over the place. This might be especially true for a project like the home entertainment system PC, because you will probably place the PC in a fairly visible location. Fortunately, there are some effective ways to hide the cables so they don't stick out like a sore thumb. Here are some ideas you may want to try:

❏ If you have carpeting, you may be able to push the Cat 5 cable under the baseboards at the edge of the room. Carpeting generally has enough flex so that the cables will slip right under the baseboard fairly easily. You'll probably need longer cables to hide them this way, however.

❏ Home supply stores often have two-piece plastic moldings that mount on the wall and can easily hide a Cat 5 cable (as well as speaker wiring). These can be painted to match your walls or existing moldings.

❑ If you need to go through a wall, you'll find that wall plates with small round holes just big enough for the Cat 5 cables are pretty handy. These plates can typically be screwed right to the wall, too, so you don't need to add a junction box underneath.

❑ In some cases, you may be able to run your Cat 5 cables between rooms by going through an attic or through a basement/crawl space.

Watch Where You Run Your Cables

Whatever you do, don't run your Cat 5 cables across the floor where people walk, since this presents a tripping hazard (as well as being dangerous to your equipment). Also, it's not a good idea to run the wires under a carpet, since people walking on top can damage the cables.

Other Types of Networking

You may see some other types of networking choices offered besides the wireless and Ethernet options I've been discussing so far. Of these alternatives, *phone line networking* is probably the most common (although it is not all that popular in reality). This is a networking scheme that functions by using some of the otherwise unused wires in your telephone jacks to transmit the network signals. Although this sounds like an ideal way to add a network to your home, there are several problems that make this less than an ideal solution:

❑ Since installers have known for years that only two wires are needed for the typical telephone connection, your jacks may not have more than the two wires connected, so there simply may not be any spare wires for networking use.

❑ Phone line networking is generally very slow. In fact, it probably would not have enough throughput for streaming multimedia content in most cases.

❑ Different brands of phone line networking equipment may not work together. If you don't buy enough equipment for future expansion when you buy the original setup, you may not be able to add onto the network in the future as your needs change.

Power Line Networking

Another type of networking that uses a similar scheme to phone line networking is power line networking. *This option sends the network signals as radio waves through the power lines in your home. Frankly, this is another one of those ideas that sounds good until you give it a bit more thought. Your power lines were never designed to handle radio frequency signals, so network speeds are severely limited.*

The Bottom Line on Networking

If you can figure out how to keep your network cables neatly tucked away out of sight, it's pretty clear that Ethernet networking is your best choice for the home entertainment system PC project. It's by far the least-expensive option and the one that offers the highest data transfer rates. It's also the most secure of any option.

On the other hand, if you just can't stomach the idea of running cables around your home, you may want to consider one of the wireless networking options. 802.11a is the fastest of these, but it is also the most expensive. 802.11b (WiFi) is less expensive, but it might not give you enough throughput for acceptable video streaming. Either one would probably work if your only requirement is to be able to share files or to stream audio.

Adding a DVD Burner

Another way to distribute multimedia content from your home entertainment system PC is on recordable DVDs, such as Verbatim DVD-R shown in Figure 6-7. DVDs offer several advantages over other types of discs, including much greater storage capacity than CDs and compatibility with most stand-alone DVD players.

Figure 6-7
Make sure you get high-quality DVD-Rs so that you can record at higher speeds.

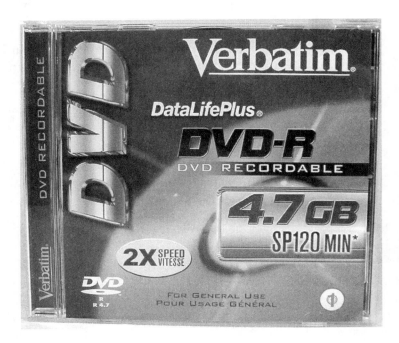

DVD-R/RW drives are similar to the CD-R/RW drives that are included on a large percentage of the desktop PCs being sold today. Most DVD-R/RW drives have the ability to record on CD-R and CD-RW in addition to recordable DVDs. You can use them for storing huge amounts of ordinary data in addition to burning your own video productions.

Which DVD Format?

There is a lot of confusion regarding which recordable DVD format to choose. Currently, there are two competing formats, and the two are incompatible with each other. In fact, the blank discs are even incompatible with drives from the opposing format, so you must use some care when buying your recordable discs.

Currently, the most popular recordable DVD format is DVD-R for write-once discs, and DVD-RW for rewritable discs. The other recordable DVD format is known as DVD+R (and DVD+RW). In researching the best option for the home entertainment system PC project, I discovered that a lot of misinformation is floating around out there. Here's the bottom line as far as I was able to determine:

❏ The DVD-R format is compatible with a higher percentage of stand-alone DVD players than any other type of recordable DVD.

❏ The first-generation DVD+R/RW drives could not actually create a DVD+R that could be read in a stand-alone DVD player. Instead, you had to use the more expensive DVD+RWs. The second-generation DVD+R/RW drives allegedly have corrected this problem.

❏ Blank DVD-Rs are considerably cheaper than other types of recordable DVDs. You do have to watch the quality of the discs you buy, however, since many of the generic discs can only be written at 1X speed, whereas the name-brand discs, like the Verbatim discs I use, can be written at 2X speed.

❏ DVD-R/RW drives tend to be less expensive than DVD+R/RW drives since their sales are higher.

Ultimately, I selected the Pioneer DVR-104 DVD-R/RW drive for the home entertainment system PC. This drive can write DVD-Rs at 2X, DVD-RWs at 1X, CD-Rs at 8X, and CD-RWs at 4X. In addition, it can read DVD-ROMs at 6X and CD-ROMs at 24X. It also supports CD text format.

Be a Careful Shopper

It really pays to shop around when you're buying a DVD-R/RW drive. At the time I'm writing this, the Pioneer DVR-104 drive ranged from a low of about $250 up to $450, depending on where I was shopping. Also, keep in mind that some vendors sell bare drives with no software. If you don't have some other software for recording DVDs, you'll definitely want to buy a drive that includes a software bundle.

Burning Your Own Mix

One of the most annoying things about buying audio CDs is simply that very few of them seem to be worth the expense. For example:

❏ Since a standard audio CD holds 74 minutes of music, why do so many CDs only use about one half of the disc?

❏ If an audio CD contains ten songs, why does it always seem like three or four of them were included just to make sure the CD had at least 35 minutes of music?

Wouldn't it be so much nicer to burn your own custom CDs that are *full* of your favorite music? After all, when you set off on a trip in your car, you may have a six- or even ten-disc CD changer, but doesn't it seem like you hear the same music over and over because the discs are too short?

Well, this is one place your home entertainment system PC can really help. Most CD players—both in the home and automotive models—can play audio CDs you record on CD-Rs. Since the DVD-R/RW drive can record these discs, you can burn your own mix for use in those players. You'll never have to endure another road trip skipping through music you want to hear or hearing the same music over and over again!

One important point you need to remember about creating audio CDs for use in stand-alone audio CD players is that those CDs must be in the standard audio CD format. This means that you can forget about packing hours of MP3s onto a disc, because most stand-alone audio CD players can't play MP3s. There are a very few newer models that support the MP3 format, but these are very rare.

Hours of Music on One Disc

There's nothing to prevent you from burning a disc full of MP3s for playback on another PC or on one of those portable MP3 disc players, however. In fact, this can be an excellent way to create discs that contain many hours of your favorite music.

Creating DVD Movies

Since we've already decided to add a DVD-R/RW drive to the home entertainment system PC, it only seems natural to want to create our own DVD movies. It turns out that the way we've configured the system makes it ideal for this use. We have plenty of processing power, a very capable video adapter, a lot of disk space, and enough memory to bring it all together.

Creating DVD movies does require one more item—the proper software. This is an area where you have many choices, but I'm going to hold off the discussion of application software until Chapter 9. For now, I'll just show you an example of one piece of software you can use to create your own DVDs. Figure 6-8 shows a sample movie being created in Pinnacle Studio 8. In this case, I've selected the option to write the movie to a DVD.

Figure 6-8
You need software such as Pinnacle Studio 8 to create DVD movies.

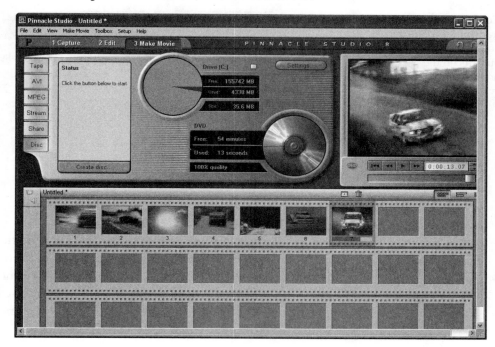

Audio and Video Signal Sharing

If you want to be able to distribute multimedia content from your home entertainment system PC to a big screen TV or to a component audio receiver, you'll need to place the PC pretty close to those components. That's not a problem in my house, but you may be in a situation where it is. In that case, you'll need a different option for sharing the audio and video signals.

Wireless Audio and Video Signal Sharing

One of the best ways to distribute audio and video signals wirelessly is the Terk Leapfrog WaveMaster 20 video distribution system I mentioned briefly in Chapter 3. This system uses radio frequencies in the 2.4 GHz band to send the audio and video signals anywhere in your home.

10 MINUTES

To use the Terk video distribution system:

1. Connect the transmitter unit to the video and audio outputs on the ATI video board's input/output block. Figure 6-9 shows the inputs on the Terk transmitter unit.

Figure 6-9
Connect this transmitter to the audio and video outputs on the home entertainment system PC.

2. Next you place the Terk receiver near the TV or audio receiver, and connect the outputs on the Terk receiver using the connections shown in Figure 6-10. Notice that the Terk receiver can connect to either the coax input or to the video input on the TV. If you use the coax input, you also need to set the Terk receiver to either channel 3 or channel 4 to match your TV.

Figure 6-10
Connect this receiver to your TV or audio receiver.

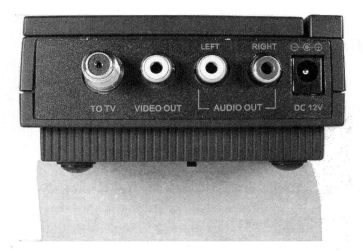

3. Both the transmitter and receiver need to be connected to power, and each has a small antenna that may have to be raised and oriented for the best picture quality. You probably won't have to raise the antennas if the transmitter and receiver are located fairly close together, but you'll want to experiment to see what produces the best results.

HEADS UP!

Add Convenience with Extra Receivers

You can add additional Terk receivers if you want to send audio or video signals to more than one location. For example, you might want to have a second receiver so that you can watch the same DVD movie in your kitchen while it is playing on the big screen TV in the living room. That way, you won't miss anything if you get up to finish making dinner.

Wired Audio and Video Signal Sharing

It is also possible to share your home entertainment system PC multimedia content by running cables instead of using a transmitter and receiver. Generally speaking, though, you'll find that this is not a particularly effective way to send signals any great distance (and you end up with the problem of unsightly cables, too). Still, if you do want to use wires to distribute the content, here are some things to consider:

❑ Audio and video signals are fairly low-voltage signals. As a result, long cable runs can cause a lot of signal deterioration—especially if you try to use cheap, unshielded cables.

❑ To avoid interference (such as hum in the audio or lines in the video), make certain that the cables are kept away from any electrical wiring and especially fluorescent lights.

❑ Video signals may need extra amplification if the picture is clear at your home entertainment system PC but fuzzy at the TV set. Places like Radio Shack and Home Depot offer video distribution amplifiers, like the RCA VH121 shown in Figure 6-11, which do an excellent job of providing a stronger, cleaner signal. Note, though, that you will need to convert the output signal from the home entertainment system PC into an RF signal to use a distribution amplifier. One way to accomplish this is to send the output through a VCR.

Figure 6-11
Video distribution amplifiers can greatly improve TV signal quality.

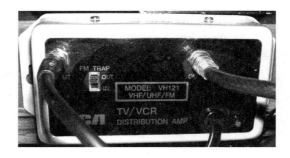

Streaming Your Content

Earlier in this chapter, I mentioned streaming video just briefly. Now I'd like to expand on that idea somewhat to explain yet another way you can distribute the multimedia entertainment from your home entertainment system PC.

If you have a home network, you already know that you can share files between different PCs quite easily. With the right application, you can also enable the other PCs on your network to display things like TV shows—even if they do not have a TV tuner card—by supplying the content from your home entertainment system PC.

The ATI All-In-Wonder Radeon 8500DV video board we selected for the home entertainment system PC project has a built-in TV tuner. This enables you to watch TV shows on your monitor or to send those signals to a big screen TV. Figure 6-12 shows an example of watching TV on the monitor.

Figure 6-12
Using the home entertainment system PC monitor to watch TV.

You may, however, want to watch those TV shows on other PCs on your network—not just on the home entertainment system PC. For that, you'll need something like SnapStream PVS (www.snapstream.com), as shown in Figure 6-13. With SnapStream PVS, your home entertainment system PC can act as a server and provide TV signals to the other PCs on your network. Those other PCs don't need a TV tuner card. All they need is to have a browser and media player installed and configured to get the TV signals from the home entertainment system PC. They don't even need a copy of SnapStream PVS.

Figure 6-13
SnapStream PVS can supply TV signals to other PCs on your network.

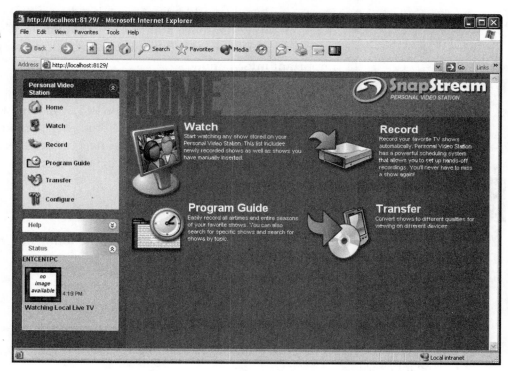

Adding a Second DVD Drive

Although this is not exactly directly related to distributing your content from your home entertainment system PC, adding a second DVD drive may be a very good idea. There are a number of reasons for this, including the following:

❑ If you ever want to make a duplicate of an existing disc, it's much easier to do if you have a second drive that can read the disc while your DVD-R/RW drive is burning the copy. That way, you won't have to first copy the source disc to your hard drive before beginning the copy.

❏ DVD-R/RW drives often are a bit slower at reading disc content than nonwritable drives. You'll want the fastest read speed possible when you're reading data discs or when you're duplicating a disc. In fact, when you're duplicating a disc, it's very important that the read speed be considerably higher than the write speed to avoid *buffer under run* problems, which can ruin the disc you're attempting to create.

❏ A second drive makes it possible to do more things at the same time. For example, you could have a writable disc in one drive, and a data disc containing reference materials in another. That way, you could be creating and storing a document while still having full access to important information.

There are many very effective ways to distribute the multimedia content that you create on your home entertainment system PC. In this chapter, I've introduced you to a number of them. As you use your home entertainment system PC, I'm sure you'll find that *sharing* the fun becomes part of the entertainment.

**TESTING
1-2-3**

At this point, you should double-check to make certain the following items have been completed:

❏ Your DVD-R/RW drive is installed correctly.

❏ Your network card is installed.

❏ Your network cabling is connected and routed so that it will not be a hazard.

❏ Your additional networking components, if any, are completely installed.

Part II

Getting More from Your PC Home Entertainment System

6:00 PM (30mins) Monday, Oct 21

Log	Stations	Titles	Actors

ORD

6:00 PM	6:30 PM
Evening News	News
KCRA 3...	KCRA 3...
News	ET
Business	NewsHour
NewsHour	Watch
NFL Football	Record
Indianapolis Col	Favorite
NFL Football	Program Details...
Indianapolis Col	Goto KNPE(5)
NewsHour	
The Simpsons	The Simpsons
The Springfield	Children of a Lesser
Evening	News
Family Feud	Family Feud
Home Imp...	Susan

Chapter 7

Accessing New Content

Tools of the Trade

To complete this chapter you will need:

An Internet connection

An amplified TV antenna or other video source

E ven the most powerful home entertainment system PC would get pretty boring if you didn't have any new content to play on it. Therefore, we'll use this chapter to take a look at some of your options for accessing new content. I think you'll be pleasantly surprised at just how many different sources of new entertainment content you can find. For example, since your home entertainment system PC is a real computer, the whole world of possibilities on the Internet is open to you. You'll find Internet radio stations, streaming video, and thousands of music files you can download for little or no cost. But the Internet isn't your only option. Because your home entertainment system PC includes a TV tuner, the whole range of over-the-air television entertainment is yours, too.

It's important to remember that even though your home entertainment system PC is actually a PC, a big part of this whole project has been ensuring that it has capabilities that are far beyond those of run-of-the-mill PCs. It's those extraordinary capabilities that give you the opportunity to access and use all the exciting entertainment options in ways you've never been able to in the past. For example, with your home entertainment system PC in control, you can now view live TV shows as is convenient for you. If you want to get a snack or answer the phone, you can simply pause the show and resume it when you're ready to continue. Want to see an instant replay of some off-the-cuff remark a politician just made? Well, that's a part of the package, too.

In this chapter, I will tell you *how* you can find the best new content, but obviously I can't tell you *where* to find the best new content—that's a moving target that depends heavily on your personal interests. Rather, I'm going to make certain that you leave this chapter knowing how to set up your home entertainment system PC so it can access what interests you. Along the way, I'll offer some suggestions to get you started, but I'm sure you'll easily find all the entertainment you can handle.

Internet Access

Before you can do anything useful on the Internet, you need to get your home entertainment system PC connected to it. Fortunately, the New Connection Wizard in Windows XP (see Figure 7-1) makes this a fairly simple and painless process.

Figure 7-1
Use the New Connection Wizard to set up your Internet connection.

1. The New Connection Wizard will start automatically the first time you click the Internet Explorer icon, but you can also choose to start the wizard manually by clicking the Start button and then choosing All Programs | Accessories | Communications | New Connection Wizard.

2. When you click the Next button, you'll be given the option to choose the type of connection you want to create, as shown in Figure 7-2. In this case, of course, you'll select the first option so that you can set up an Internet connection.

Figure 7-2
Choose the Connect
To The Internet
option.

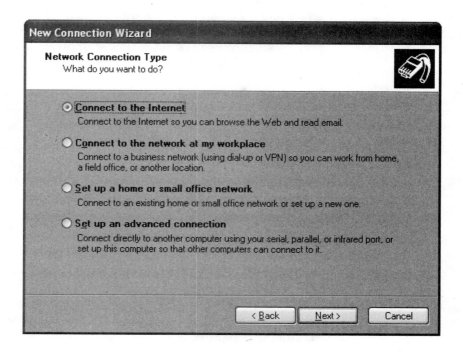

3. After you've selected the option to set up an Internet connection, click Next to continue. At this point, you need to decide *how* you want to connect to the Internet. This decision affects what happens during the rest of the process. The following list describes your three options:

❑ **Choose from a list of Internet services providers (ISPs)**   Select this option if you don't already have an Internet account and want to choose from a list of providers who serve your area. In most cases, this list will primarily consist of the big national ISPs such as EarthLink, MSN, or AOL. You can also choose this option if you have an existing account with one of the national ISPs, but be careful that you do not inadvertently sign up for a new account.

❑ **Set up my connection manually**   This is your best option if you have an existing Internet account—especially if it is with one of the smaller, local ISPs who probably won't make Microsoft's list of ISPs. You'll need to know your username, password, and dial-up phone number, at a minimum. You may also need to know some technical details if your ISP requires you to enter specific settings such as DNS addresses.

❑ **Use the CD I got from an ISP**   Select this option if you have a CD-ROM from an ISP such as EarthLink or AOL. You may want to choose this if you want to take advantage of one of those free trial offers (but make certain that you note the important details of the offer, such as what you must do to cancel your account—some ISPs make this almost impossible once the free trial period has ended).

From this point onward, the screens you see and the choices you must make will be determined by which option you have selected in the preceding list. Because so many variables are involved, it's really not possible for me describe every scenario or to anticipate which selections you'll make from the options that are offered. Fortunately, the New Connection Wizard explains your choices quite clearly and is very easy to follow. So, rather than attempt to step through the New Connection Wizard any further, I'll move on to a brief discussion of the Internet connection options you may want to consider.

Internet Connection Options

Let's take a quick look at the Internet connection options you may have available, along with the pluses and minuses of each with respect to your home entertainment system PC.

Your Options Will Vary

There are a number of different methods for connecting to the Internet. The options that are available to you depend almost entirely on your location. Unfortunately, the most desirable options are also the ones that are the most difficult to obtain, since they are totally dependent on whether anyone is offering that particular service in your area.

DSL and Cable

Both DSL and cable are known as "always on" Internet connections, since your PC is always connected and you don't have to wait for a modem to dial a number and connect. This always-on nature is both a boon and a potential problem. Eliminating the wait to connect means that you will have a much easier time using the Internet, since you can just click and go. But having a persistent connection also means that your home entertainment system PC is more vulnerable to attacks from computer viruses and crackers. I personally would never connect to the Internet over any type of connection without effective and up-to-date antivirus software, such as Panda Antivirus Platinum (see Figure 7-3) in place and functioning (www.pandasoftware.com).

Figure 7-3
Make certain that you have dependable antivirus software running whenever you are connected to the Internet.

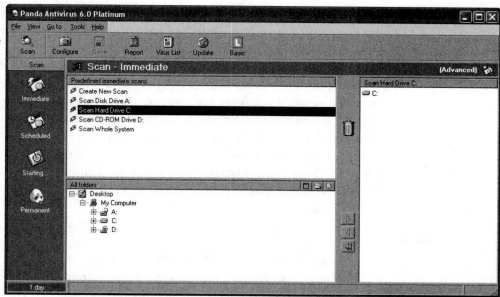

If you have the option of choosing either DSL or cable for connecting your home entertainment system PC to the Internet, I really can't imagine why you would want to consider anything else. But if you're among the vast majority for whom neither of those is available, I've also included a section that covers your remaining choices.

DSL

Digital Subscriber Line (DSL) is a type of Internet connection that uses your existing telephone line to provide high-speed access. In most cases, the DSL service offering is technically known as *asynchronous DSL (ADSL)*, which indicates the fact that you can download data much faster than you can upload data. For the home entertainment system PC, this is actually a perfect situation, since it means that you'll be able to download new content much faster.

A DSL connection offers sufficient speed to watch fairly high-quality streaming video from the Internet on your home entertainment system PC. Essentially, this means that a DSL connection enables you to watch Internet TV broadcasts that can have near over-the-air broadcast quality. A DSL line also enables you to easily download various music files and to listen to Internet radio stations.

Because the DSL connection works over your existing phone line—but doesn't interrupt it—you don't need a second phone line for your Internet connection. In addition, the monthly charge for a DSL connection typically (but not always) also covers the cost of your Internet access, so a DSL connection may compare quite favorably with the cost of a separate phone line for a dial-up connection along with an account with an ISP.

Unfortunately, DSL service is still far from readily available outside a relatively small geographical area concentrated close to major cities. Basically, most DSL service is limited to those areas that are less than three miles from the telephone company's central office (and this is measured by the distance the wire must go—not by your actual distance).

If you can get DSL service, you're likely to see connection speeds that range from 5 to 50 times that of dial-up connections. The speed varies according to your distance from the central office, with lower speeds the further away you are from that location.

Cable

Internet access through cable TV lines typically offers similar speeds and costs as with DSL service. Depending on your area, you may have one or both options available to you, and either one would be an excellent choice compared to a dial-up connection.

Cable Access Considerations

Cable access to the Internet does have certain disadvantages compared to DSL access. The most important one seems to be that cable access can slow down considerably if a large number of people in your area are attempting to access the Internet at the same time. The reason for this is simply that with cable, everyone in your neighborhood is essentially sharing one connection, whereas with DSL, you have your own dedicated connection to the Internet.

Other Connection Options

If you are going to all the time, expense, and work to build your home entertainment system PC, it's kind of frustrating to realize that if you don't have DSL or cable available, you're quite limited in the types of entertainment content you can access through the Internet. Let's take a quick look at the options that may be your only choices.

Dial-Up

A dial-up connection is one that uses a modem to literally dial a phone number and communicate using a bunch of funny tones sent over standard phone lines. Unlike DSL, which is a digital service, dial-up connections are analog and far slower. Unfortunately, though, dial-up connections are by far the most common type of Internet connection that is available in most areas. Dial-up connections range from about 24 Kbps (kilobits per second) to 53 Kbps, but connection speed is seldom consistent from one call to the next.

Dial-up connections are slow for several reasons:

❑ Being analog, they are limited by the number of tones that can be sent reliably over standard phone lines.

❑ They're subject to interference with line noise.

❑ The FCC limits the speed of dial-up connections to prevent them from causing problems with the voice network.

At first glance, dial-up connections might seem like the cheapest method of connecting to the Internet. But since they require the use of the entire phone line, it's not all that practical to use a dial-up connection very much without paying for a second phone line just for your computer. If you add up the cost of a separate phone line and the cost of an Internet access account, dial-up connections can cost nearly as much as some of the speedier alternatives.

If a dial-up connection is your only option, you probably won't be downloading a lot of content from the Internet to your home entertainment system PC. Frankly, there isn't really a lot of content that is compact enough to make downloading it via a dial-up connection very appealing.

ISDN

Integrated Services Digital Network (ISDN) is a fairly expensive step up from a dial-up connection, but it does offer higher-bandwidth and more-reliable connections compared to dial-up. ISDN is a digital service that typically offers 64 Kbps for a single channel or 128 Kbps for two channels. This is faster than a dial-up connection, but far slower than either DSL or cable.

ISDN connections require a separate, special phone line. Depending on the *terminal adapter (TA)* that you use, it may be possible to have two voice circuits that can be used at the same time as your data connection, but I've never found this feature to work very well.

ISDN service is almost always a metered service. That is, the typical contract provides a certain amount of time per month and then you pay for any time you use above that. Unfortunately, ISDN service providers often take every possible advantage they can in counting up your connect time. First, many of them bill in one-minute increments, so even a five-second call eats up a minute of time. Next, they count each of the two channels separately, so a 100-hour-per-month allotment is actually cut down to 50 hours if you use both channels. Finally, the per-minute charge is also doubled in most cases, since each channel is counted separately. Consequently, using an ISDN connection to download a large amount of content from the Internet can quickly become a very expensive proposition.

As an aside, I'd like to point out another reason why subscribing to ISDN is probably not a good idea. Since ISDN is far more profitable to the phone company than DSL, the phone companies have little incentive to supply DSL service in areas where people have ISDN lines. Technically, both ISDN and DSL share similar distance restrictions, but there are some other minor line-quality issues that may affect your ability to get one or the other in some cases.

Satellite Internet

Another option you may want to consider is satellite Internet. This is a fairly expensive way to access the Internet, but it does offer the option of relatively high-speed access and is available almost anywhere (as long as you are allowed to have a dish antenna installed, that is).

There are two types of satellite Internet service:

❏ One-way satellite service sends content to your PC via a satellite link, but relies on a standard dial-up connection to send data from your PC to the Internet. As a result, downloads are much faster than uploads. Downloads approach the lower end of DSL speeds, but uploads are no faster than dial-up connections.

❏ Two-way satellite service uses the satellite link for both uploads and downloads (although upload speed is typically more like ISDN speed). Downloads are similar to one-way satellite.

Both types of satellite Internet access typically require a fairly substantial upfront investment in equipment and installation (you aren't allowed to install the equipment yourself). In addition, the monthly cost is often higher than for other types of Internet access. Two-way satellite access costs more than one-way, although you do have to factor in the cost of an extra phone line with one-way satellite.

Several different companies provide satellite Internet access. To find out more about what is available, you might want to check out the following links:

❏ www.earthlink.net
❏ www.direcpc.com
❏ www.cband.net

Finding a Spot for Your Dish

One potential problem you may encounter with satellite Internet access is simply finding a location where you can have the dish installed. For satellite Internet access, you need a dish that is approximately one meter across, and it must have a clear view of the southern sky. Obviously, this could be a difficult requirement for most apartment dwellers, but even some homeowners may have difficulty finding an appropriate spot for the dish.

Finding Your Web Content

Okay, so you've figured out the best type of Internet access for your home entertainment system PC, now you need to figure out where to find some entertaining content to make it all worthwhile. In the days of Napster, finding music files to download was pretty easy, but things have become a bit more complicated since that service was shut down. There are many types of content available if you know where to look.

The Issues of Online Content Distribution

One of the most contentious issues involving the Internet seems to be that of copyrights. Content creators want users to pay for what they download, while many users seem to feel that all entertainment should be available for free. I obviously can't resolve the deep dispute between these two camps in a brief few words, but I do think that there is some room for compromise. Clearly, making a certain amount of content available for free encourages the consumer to sample a product and hopefully buy more in the future. But those who want everything for free simply don't seem to understand that there has to be some incentive for creative people to do the work of creating new content.

Fortunately, there are people who understand the issues involved. They're the ones who create and maintain the web sites where consumers can legally download content that musicians, artists, movie makers, and so on are making available for free (or for a small fee). By respecting the rights of the content creators, these people make it possible for the rest of us to find entertainment we can download to our home entertainment system PCs.

Finding the Legal Sites

There is, however, just one problem with trying to figure out where you can find the sites that are currently providing the type of entertainment content you want—the Internet is constantly changing, and sites that seem like the absolute best today may be gone tomorrow. From past experience, I know that in any list of ten web sites I might recommend in one of my books, as many as three or four may disappear between the time I write the book and when you read it. Not only is this a problem for me, but it's also frustrating for you when you attempt to visit one of those great sites I've recommended.

My solution to this problem is to tell you about the best Internet search tool I've ever encountered—Copernic Agent Professional (see Figure 7-4). You'll find Copernic Agent Professional at www.copernic.com (where you'll also find Copernic Agent Basic and Copernic Agent Personal).

Figure 7-4
Copernic Agent
Professional can find
the files you want.

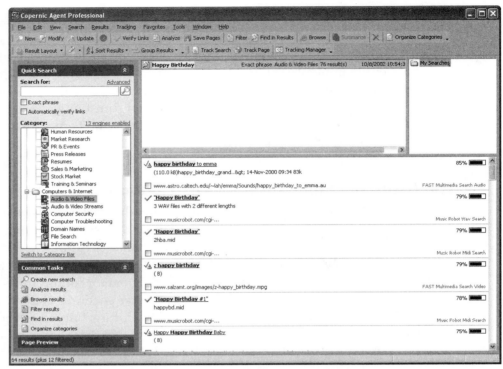

All the Copernic Agent versions function in a similar manner. When you
want to find something on the Internet, you choose the appropriate category,
enter your search terms, specify the search parameters, and begin the search.
Copernic Agent then uses powerful techniques to query a whole raft of search
engines at the same time. As the results are returned, Copernic Agent
consolidates and ranks the results so that you are left with a list of the best
matches from all the different search engines. Notice that in Figure 7-4 I asked
Copernic Agent Professional to find audio and video files using the search term
"happy birthday." In a very short time, Copernic Agent Professional found 76
valid matches of various audio and video files I could download to my home
entertainment system PC.

As handy as Copernic Agent's search capabilities are, they would soon
become as useless as any list of printed links I could offer if it weren't for one very
important feature that is included in the program. Whenever you start Copernic
Agent, the program first updates its list of search engines so that you will get the
best possible results from your searches. As Figure 7-5 shows, Copernic Agent
Professional used 13 different search engines to find the "happy birthday" audio
and video files I wanted.

Figure 7-5
In this category,
Copernic Agent
Professional combines
the results from 13
search engines.

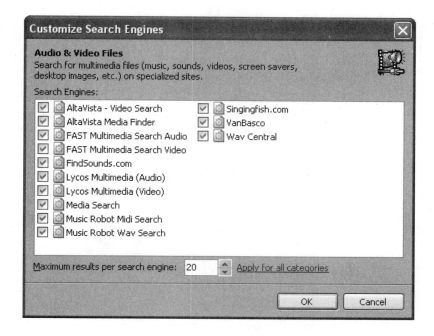

You don't, of course, have to use Copernic Agent to find what you want on the Internet. You can go to the individual search engines that Copernic Agent uses and do your own searches at each of them. Certainly, the search engine sites would rather have you there in person so that you would be looking at all of the ads their pages contain. Personally, I'd rather have Copernic Agent do it for me.

TV Signals

If you want to see a broad array of entertainment, there's nothing else that can compare to television in all of its various forms. That's why our home entertainment system PC has a feature that you won't find on very many ordinary PCs—a TV tuner. Let's take a closer look at the TV options our home entertainment system PC provides.

Over-the-Air TV

Long before anyone even dreamed of personal computers, TV broadcasts reached homes through over-the-air signals. Television remains one of the most popular forms of entertainment today even in an era of extremely powerful and capable PCs. It's only natural, then, that our home entertainment system PC is equipped to receive local over-the-air TV broadcasts.

Unless you happen to live in an area with extremely powerful TV signals, the TV tuner in your home entertainment system PC will need some extra help to be able to pick up over-the-air TV signals. That help comes in the form of an amplified antenna like the Terk unit shown in Figure 7-6. Incidentally, I sampled several different amplified indoor TV antennas before choosing this one. None of the other brands I tried provided nearly as clear a picture as the Terk antenna, and certainly none looked as good sitting on my home entertainment center.

Figure 7-6
You'll need an amplified TV antenna for acceptable over-the-air TV signals.

One important feature to watch for when you are buying an amplified indoor TV antenna is to make certain that the antenna has a coaxial cable connection rather than the old-fashioned flat ribbon cable. High-performance PCs can cause a lot of signal interference with antennas that use those flat, unshielded cables.

TV Signals from Your Satellite Receiver

If you have a satellite TV receiver, you'll no doubt want to connect your home entertainment system PC to that receiver. To do so, you may need a splitter similar to the one shown in Figure 7-7. Splitters like this come in a number of different configurations—the choice of which depends on how many different components you want to connect.

Figure 7-7
Use a splitter to connect more than one device to the same signal source.

Although the labels on most splitters seem to indicate otherwise, I've found that I can also use a splitter to combine signals from a couple of sources. For example, if you want to receive over-the-air TV signals as well as satellite TV signals on your home entertainment system PC, you can plug the amplified indoor TV antenna and the satellite TV receiver into the splitter, and then connect it to the TV signal input on your home entertainment system PC. Keep in mind, though, that your satellite receiver must be set to a channel that is not available over the air in your local area—otherwise, you'll encounter too much signal interference. In that case, you may need to buy a switch box and manually select the signal you want to watch.

Cable TV

Hooking up your cable TV connection to your home entertainment system PC is very similar to hooking up a satellite TV connection. In both cases, you connect the coax cable to the RF input on the home entertainment system PC TV tuner. Likewise, you may need to use a splitter if you want to hook up more than one receiver.

One important difference between watching satellite TV and cable TV on your home entertainment system PC is that you may be able to tune different cable channels using the TV tuner in your PC. If your cable is the type that connects directly to a TV set rather than going through an external tuning box, this will almost certainly be the case. If, on the other hand, your cable system uses an external box that does the channel selections, you'll be limited to whichever channel is currently selected by that box.

Recorded Content from Your VCR

If you're like most people, you probably have a VCR and a bunch of videotapes. The tapes might be movies you've recorded, favorite TV shows, or even recordings of family events such as vacations, birthday parties, weddings, and so on. If so, you'll probably want to be able to view your old tapes on your home entertainment system PC. In fact, since your home entertainment system PC can easily record your tapes to DVDs or VCDs, you may even want to edit the tapes to create your own masterpieces.

Most VCRs offer composite video and audio output options. Some of them also offer S-Video as a higher quality option. Either way, using the composite video or the S-Video connection will produce a cleaner signal than using the RF output from the VCR. In addition, using either of these video options means that you don't have to hook up yet another source to the splitter, since the ATI All-In-Wonder Radeon 8500DV video card we selected for the home entertainment system PC project has both composite video and S-Video inputs on its external connection block. In Figure 7-8, I'm using the composite video input to accept the signals from my VCR.

Figure 7-8
The external input block provides a convenient method of connecting your VCR.

Incidentally, the audio signal is separate from the video signal regardless of whether you are using composite video or S-Video. You must connect the audio outputs from the VCR to the audio inputs on the home entertainment system PC in order to hear the sound from the video tape.

One thing I haven't discussed yet is just how you can use all of this new entertainment content on your home entertainment system PC. I'll bring all of that together in Chapter 9, in which I'll show you the different pieces of software you'll need to make everything work properly. Fortunately, much of the software you'll need typically comes with the various components you've bought to assemble your system. But if you've been building your home entertainment system PC by upgrading an existing PC, you may not have quite the same mix of software in your collection. That's why I'm going to cover the software all together in one place—so you'll only have to look there to see what you need.

TESTING
1-2-3

At this point, you should double-check to make certain the following items have been completed:

❑ Your Internet connection is properly configured.

❑ Your video sources are hooked up and functioning.

Chapter 8

Nice Extras You'll Want to Have

Tools of the Trade

To complete this chapter you'll need:

Logitech Cordless Freedom Optical keyboard and mouse

ATI All-In-Wonder Radeon 8500DV RF remote control

(or another remote control that works with your home entertainment system PC)

An uninterruptible power supply (UPS)

Optional—a Pocket PC and SnapStream Pocket PVS

Optional—a wireless network card for your Pocket PC

Optional—NetOp Remote Control

Optional—game controllers

Now that you have your home entertainment system PC almost entirely together, it's time to think about some of those things that can add just a bit of extra convenience to the whole system. These are things that you could live without, I suppose, but they're certainly worth thinking about. After all, you do want to get the most enjoyment possible from your home entertainment system PC, don't you?

This chapter is all about fun stuff. That is, something like a wireless trackball may seem a bit over the top, but you aren't going to have to do much to convince people just how cool your home entertainment system PC really is once you start scrolling around the screen with that wireless trackball. So, keep an open mind, and we'll have a look at some of the neatest add-ons you can find.

Wireless Input

I don't know about your home, but at my place, one of the biggest objections to adding a PC to the home entertainment system was the possibility of having a whole bunch of extra wires all over the place. Oh, the various cables behind the PC aren't that much of a problem since they can be hidden away inside the cabinet, but the keyboard and mouse cables are a different story. Whenever you're using the home entertainment system PC with the keyboard on your lap and the mouse on the end table, those wires are right out there in the open—potentially right where they need to be to trip someone—but definitely where they give the whole thing a messy, "techie" appearance.

But even if the sight of the keyboard and mouse cables isn't an issue at your house, I'll bet you're none too happy with the length of those cables. Unless you buy some extension cables, it's awfully hard to sit back on the sofa with your keyboard in your lap. Let's look at some better options.

Wireless Keyboard

Face it—you really can't have a PC without some method of inputting data. Although voice recognition is certainly much more useful than it was even a few years ago, most of that input is still through a keyboard. The days of the *Star Trek* intelligent computer that can determine what you want by listening to your conversations and reacting appropriately are still some time in the future.

Figure 8-1 shows the Logitech Cordless Freedom Optical keyboard that I selected for the home entertainment system PC project (www.logitech.com). This slick black keyboard not only is wireless, but also is quite good looking and has a number of extra functions that really add to its usefulness. For example, the large round dial at the top center of this keyboard is actually a volume control that you can use to adjust the volume of the sounds coming from the home entertainment system PC.

Figure 8-1
This Logitech wireless keyboard is a perfect addition to the home entertainment system PC.

TIPS OF THE TRADE

Don't Worry, It Will Work Right Away

Although this might seem obvious, the Logitech Cordless Freedom Optical keyboard is functional as soon as you plug in its receiver and press the Connect buttons on the receiver and the keyboard. That is, you can use this keyboard without first plugging in an ordinary wired keyboard. You will need to install some drivers that Logitech provides in order to activate all the special keys on this keyboard, but you'll be able to use the basic keyboard functions immediately.

You'll find this wireless keyboard especially handy if you use a large screen TV as the display for your home entertainment system PC. Although Logitech states that the keyboard should work within 6 feet of the receiver, I've actually used it over 20 feet away, so it should have plenty of range to enable you to sit back on your sofa or easy chair and type away in comfort. And, as I mentioned earlier, you won't have to worry about someone tripping over the cord to your keyboard, either.

Wireless Mouse

A wireless keyboard is great, but if you're going to skip the keyboard cable, how about skipping the mouse cable, too? There's no sense in having some ordinary old wired mouse when you can have a cordless one and get rid of yet another of those pesky cables that serve to make everything look so messy.

Figure 8-2 shows the cordless mouse I'm using for the home entertainment system PC. This beauty is right in the package with the Logitech Cordless Freedom Optical keyboard, so the two make a great team.

Figure 8-2
This Logitech cordless mouse eliminates another messy cable.

In addition to being cordless, the home entertainment system PC mouse is also an optical mouse. Optical mice have a huge advantage over mechanical ones because they have no moving parts to get gummed up with lint, cat hair, or spilled sodas. If you're still using one of those old-fashioned mice with the little rubber ball inside, you certainly know what I mean. With an optical mouse, you never end up with a sticky, jumpy mouse pointer, so using the mouse once again becomes enjoyable rather than a constant aggravation.

Incidentally, the cordless optical mouse that Logitech includes with the Cordless Freedom Optical keyboard is similar but not identical to the Logitech Cordless Optical Mouse that you can buy separately. In fact, the one that is included with the keyboard is superior to the stand-alone one because it has an additional, programmable thumb button on its left side. You might, however, prefer the stand-alone Cordless Optical Mouse if you happen to be left-handed, since that unit is symmetrical for use with either hand.

Wireless Trackball

As handy as a cordless optical mouse may be, it may not be the best choice for your home entertainment system PC if you want to use the keyboard and pointing device while sitting on your sofa. Quite simply, you probably don't have a convenient flat surface that will work very well for moving the mouse. Even though an optical mouse does not require nearly as even a surface as a mechanical mouse, it wasn't really designed for rolling across the cushions on your living room sofa.

Figure 8-3 shows an excellent alternative when you want to move the mouse pointer without moving a mouse. This is the Logitech Cordless Optical TrackMan—a cordless, optical trackball.

Figure 8-3
This Logitech trackball may work better than a mouse when you're sitting on your sofa.

A trackball is somewhat similar to an upside-down mouse. Rather than moving the whole mouse body around, you use your fingers to roll the ball in the direction you want the mouse pointer to move. As you can imagine, this makes it much easier to control the mouse pointer when you're sitting comfortably in your favorite easy chair.

In addition to all the buttons you would normally find on a mouse, the Logitech Cordless Optical TrackMan includes a bunch of extra buttons that are designed to make using the trackball even easier. For example, one button is the *drag-lock* button, which you press to begin dragging an object onscreen. When you press the same button a second time, the object is released. As a result, you don't have to hold a button down the whole time while you are dragging it.

Remote Controls

Does anyone use a television set without a remote control anymore? Do you even know how to change the channels on your TV without using the remote control? No cheating now!

If your home entertainment system PC is really going to be a part of your television watching, it simply is going to have to emulate your TV in a number of important ways. And, of course, enabling you to change channels, adjust the volume, and all the other everyday TV functions via a remote control is an important part of that whole experience, isn't it? In other words, your home entertainment system PC just isn't going to fit in unless you can pick up a remote control and channel surf.

In choosing the ATI All-In-Wonder Radeon 8500DV video board for the home entertainment system PC, one of the important considerations was the included remote control. This is a video board that knows how to act like a TV set.

But if you selected a different video board or perhaps a stand-alone TV tuner for your version of the home entertainment system PC, you may not have a remote control. Well, never fear, because that's an easily solved deficiency. There are two different types of remote controls: RF remote controls and infrared remote controls.

RF Remote Controls

RF remote controls (like the ATI remote control shown in Figure 8-4) use radio signals to communicate your commands. Of the two types of remote controls, RF remotes are the best, for one very simple reason—they don't have to be aimed right at the receiver to work. In fact, RF remotes generally don't even have to be in the same room as the receiver. You'll really appreciate this feature if you're distributing the TV signals from your home entertainment system PC wirelessly, and don't have the PC in your living room near your big screen TV.

Figure 8-4
This remote control can make your home entertainment system PC act like a real TV set.

The RF Remote As An Add-On

You may be wondering why I'm mentioning the ATI RF remote control since it was included with the home entertainment system PC's video board. Well, ATI realized that not everyone would be buying the All-In-Wonder Radeon 8500DV video board, so some people wouldn't be getting the remote control. As a result, ATI actually sells the RF remote control separately, so you can buy one for use with whatever video board and TV tuner card you may have selected. The RF remote control includes a small radio receiver that plugs into a USB port, and it includes directions for use with different types of hardware.

Infrared Remote Controls

Infrared remote controls (like the Pinnacle remote control shown in Figure 8-5) look pretty much the same as RF remote controls, but they don't work the same way.

Figure 8-5
This Pinnacle remote control only works with the Pinnacle PCTV card.

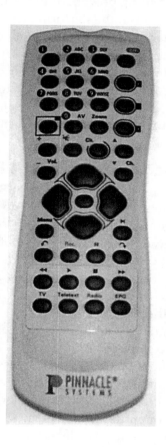

Infrared remote controls must be pointed at the receiver, and if anything is in the way, they are easily blocked—preventing them from working properly. The reason is that infrared remote controls use an infrared light beam rather than a radio signal to carry your commands to the receiver.

Although the Pinnacle infrared remote control is not available separately, it does come in the box with the Pinnacle PCTV tuner card, so it might be a good choice if you're upgrading an existing PC and you plan on having the home entertainment system PC in the same room as the rest of your home entertainment equipment. You'll only be able to use it with the Pinnacle PCTV card, of course, but that card does offer an inexpensive way to add a TV tuner and a remote to the PC you're upgrading.

Partnering with Your Pocket PC

I have to admit that I'm a big fan of the Pocket PC. With it, I'm able to carry some real computing power around in my pocket so that I can send off a quick e-mail message, check the performance of my investments, jot down some ideas I've just thought of, and even read an electronic book pretty much anywhere. I also know that my Pocket PC can interact with my desktop PC in a number of very interesting ways that might not occur to most people. It's only natural, then, that I devote a small amount of space to telling you about some of the ways that your Pocket PC and your home entertainment system PC can partner to enhance your entertainment universe even further.

Streaming Video on Your Pocket PC

You may recall my mention of the SnapStream PVS application in Chapter 6. This is a program that enables you not only to record video content on your home entertainment system PC, but also to provide a video stream to other PCs on your network. Essentially, SnapStream PVS enables your home entertainment system PC to become a TV broadcast server so that all the PCs on your network can play back TV shows, movies, or whatever other content you've recorded—without the need for individual TV tuners or any other special equipment in those other PCs.

Imagine, though, just how useful it might be if you could download a recorded show to your Pocket PC and then watch that show on your Pocket PC. You could then do things like pass the time on a long flight by viewing a movie instead of listening to some boring stranger tell you all about his new idea for some multilevel marketing scheme. You could spend the time riding to work on the commuter train watching your daily lesson for a class you're taking via TV from your local college. Or maybe you want to spend the time watching a TV language course in anticipation of a foreign trip that you're planning. All of these scenarios are not only possible, but are excellent examples of how your Pocket PC and your home entertainment system PC can team up to give you something more than either one could do on its own.

If you own a Pocket PC, you already know that storage space is always at a premium on those types of devices. Storing large amounts of multimedia content seems almost impossible. Fortunately, SnapStream has a way around this problem. Rather than storing desktop-quality recordings on your Pocket PC, SnapStream converts those recordings to a much smaller size format specifically intended for the Pocket PC's display. Depending on the quality level you choose, you may be able to store as much as an hour of recorded TV on a 64MB memory card. Just think—a fairly inexpensive 128MB memory card is large enough to hold most full-length feature films!

Don't Forget Pocket PVS

By the way, SnapStream offers an add-on to SnapStream PVS called Pocket PVS. You use this add-on to compress and transfer the video recordings to your Pocket PC. You then view the recorded programs using the Windows Media Player on your Pocket PC.

Wireless Pocket PC

Okay, so you've already decided that you want a wireless keyboard and mouse for your home entertainment system PC. Why, then, would you want to have to plug your Pocket PC into some cable? After all, isn't that just about as bad as having a keyboard and mouse cable strung across your living room?

Fortunately, adding wireless access to your home entertainment system PC from your Pocket PC is quite easy. You may even find that wireless access is both far more convenient and faster than the standard USB connection, too. Let's take a look at a couple of options you may want to consider.

Pocket PC Bluetooth

In many ways, Bluetooth connections and Pocket PCs seem like the perfect pair. Pocket PCs are powerful little computers, but a part of their small size comes from the very compact batteries they use. Power conservation is an absolute necessity if you want to get any reasonable amount of battery life.

Of all the wireless connection options, Bluetooth is by far the champion in terms of squeezing out the most results with the least amount of power drain. In fact, a Pocket PC Bluetooth card like the Socket model shown in Figure 8-6 (www.socketcom.com) uses something in the area of one-tenth the power that is consumed by a WiFi card.

Figure 8-6
This Socket Bluetooth card enables your Pocket PC to talk to your home entertainment system PC using very little power.

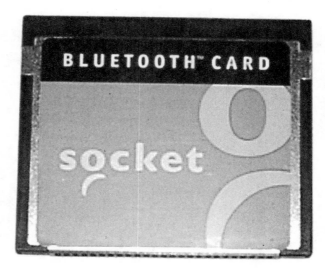

Bluetooth, of course, has a much shorter range than WiFi (802.11b). Still, you should be able to get a reliable connection between your Pocket PC and your home entertainment system PC within about 30–50 feet in the typical home environment. (Refer to Chapter 6 for more on Bluetooth.)

Consider the Motherboard Bluetooth Option

If you do decide to use Bluetooth, remember that MSI offers the optional Bluetooth module for its KT3 Ultra2-R motherboard we selected for this project. The Bluetooth module is certainly the most convenient way to add Bluetooth capability to your home entertainment system PC.

The Socket Bluetooth card for the Pocket PC fits a standard Type 1 CF (CompactFlash) slot, so it will work in any Pocket PC that has either a Type 1 or Type 2 CF slot. The card does not fit the smaller SD (Secure Digital) expansion slots found on some Pocket PCs, however, so make sure your Pocket PC has a CF slot before you buy the Bluetooth card or the Bluetooth module for the motherboard.

Pocket PC WiFi

Even though Bluetooth is a great choice for a low-power wireless connection between your Pocket PC and your home entertainment system PC, it's not necessarily the best choice in every situation. For example, if you've installed a WiFi network so that your home entertainment system PC can communicate with your other PCs, you'll probably want to use the same type of connection for your Pocket PC as well.

Figure 8-7 shows the Proxim Harmony WiFi card I use in my Pocket PC (www.proxim.com). Since this card communicates using the standard 802.11b wireless networking protocols, it is completely compatible with my WiFi network.

Figure 8-7
Use this Proxim Harmony 802.11b card to add your Pocket PC to your wireless network.

I do have to be more careful in watching the power consumption when I have the WiFi card plugged into my Pocket PC. Fortunately, it's easy to turn the radio off or even to simply pop the card out of my Pocket PC when I'm not using it. Even with the added power drain, I still like using the WiFi connection—especially when I'm transferring large files to or from my Pocket PC—since the speed is far better than if I use the standard USB connection.

The Proxim Harmony 802.11b card requires a Type 2 CF slot, so it won't fit into the narrower Type 1 CF slot that is found on some Pocket PCs. Be sure to check compatibility before you buy.

NetOp Remote Control

Next I'm going to show you a program that really makes a wireless connection between your Pocket PC and your home entertainment system PC all worthwhile. NetOp Remote Control (www.netop.com) enables your Pocket PC to control your home entertainment system PC using that wireless connection. For example, Figure 8-8 shows the control panel for the ATI TV application as viewed on my Pocket PC's screen. I can easily control the TV tuner just by tapping on the screen of my Pocket PC.

Figure 8-8
NetOp Remote Control makes your Pocket PC into a remote control for your home entertainment system PC.

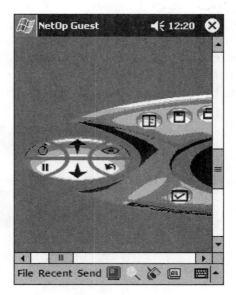

In addition to controlling individual applications, you can start programs, change settings (such as the volume), and just generally use your Pocket PC to take charge of your home entertainment system PC through NetOp Remote Control. Figure 8-9 shows how my Pocket PC's screen looks just after I've clicked the home entertainment system PC's Start button by tapping it on the Pocket PC's screen.

Figure 8-9
Here I've opened
the home
entertainment system
PC's Start menu from
the Pocket PC.

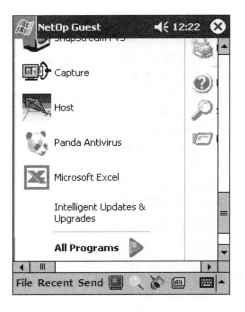

Finally, I thought you might like to see one more view of the home entertainment system PC desktop as shown on the Pocket PC. In Figure 8-10, I clicked the Full Screen button in the Pocket PC NetOp Guest program. This enables you to see the entire home entertainment system PC desktop shrunk down to fit the Pocket PC's screen. You can then use the zoom control to quickly focus in on a specific area of the home entertainment system PC's desktop. Sometimes this may be faster than using the scroll bars to move around the screen.

Figure 8-10
You can even view
the entire home
entertainment system
PC desktop on the
Pocket PC's screen.

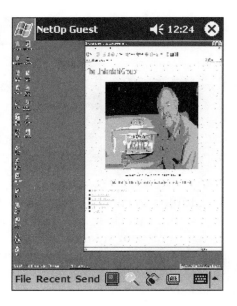

As I mentioned at the beginning of this section, I'm a big fan of the Pocket PC, and I see a partnership between it and your home entertainment system PC as a natural. If you don't already have a Pocket PC, at least you should now have a better understanding of how the two systems can complement each other.

UPS

At its heart, your home entertainment system PC really is a PC. If it's going to serve you well, it needs a very steady diet of clean, dependable power. If the power goes out—even for a second—you could lose data. In fact, if the power is lost at just the worst possible time, it's even possible to severely damage the very files that enable your home entertainment system PC to function.

To protect your home entertainment system PC and all the various files it contains, I strongly recommend that you connect it to an *uninterruptible power supply (UPS)*. A UPS maintains a steady flow of power to your home entertainment system PC by supplying power from rechargeable batteries whenever the power goes out—even for a fraction of a second. Thus, your PC never misses a beat, because it always has the power it needs.

In addition to supplying continuous power, a UPS also protects your home entertainment system PC from high-voltage spikes that can come into your home through the power lines. These spikes can be caused by lightning, by someone in your neighborhood using an arc welder, or even by someone running into a power pole. Regardless of their cause, spikes can be deadly to a PC. And even if they don't damage any of the components physically, spikes can cause changes in your files—possibly rendering them useless!

A UPS is rated in what are known as volt-amps (VA). These are roughly equivalent to watts, although PC power supplies use power a little differently from other types of equipment, so the equivalence is not exact. Higher VA ratings enable a UPS to power more equipment at the same time or to power the same equipment during a longer power outage.

Your home entertainment system PC needs a UPS of at least 350 VA, but if you can find a 500 VA or 600 VA unit, you'll be adding some extra protection. If you plan on plugging a monitor or big screen TV into the UPS, you'll need a larger unit. Check the wattage rating for the monitor or big screen TV to see how much additional capacity you will need.

Watch That Printer

I recommend that you do not plug your printer (if you have one) into the UPS. You can always hold off running any print jobs until the power returns. Besides, laser printers draw so much power that they'll quickly deplete the batteries on even the largest home UPS. Inkjet printers don't use as much power as laser printers, but there's no real reason to connect them to the UPS.

I'm not going to recommend a specific brand of UPS because you most likely will buy your UPS off the shelf at a local store, and I've never found that brand mattered very much. In addition, I've found that some of the less-expensive "generic" UPS models are actually made by the big-name UPS manufacturers, and even include the same UPS monitoring software inside the box.

Game Controllers

If you like to play computer games, your home entertainment system PC is the perfect game platform. It has the computing power, the graphics, and the sound system to really make your games come alive. But it is missing one important element that makes playing games fun—game controllers. There is an awful lot lost when you try to fly an airplane or drive a racecar with your keyboard and mouse. Somehow the whole experience just comes up lacking compared to when you have specially designed game controllers.

Logitech, the manufacturer of the cordless keyboard and mouse being used on the home entertainment system PC, also makes a line of really great game controllers (www.logitech.com). Figure 8-11 shows the WingMan Extreme Digital 3D joystick, which will make any type of flight simulator a whole lot more realistic.

Figure 8-11
You really need a joystick to enjoy flying games.

On the other hand, if your favorite type of game is auto racing, you may want to consider something like the WingMan Formula Force GP shown in Figure 8-12. To make game play even more realistic, this game controller includes a set of pedals so you can more easily control acceleration and braking.

Figure 8-12
A steering wheel makes racing games a lot more fun.

Finally, you might want to consider something like the WingMan Cordless Rumblepad shown in Figure 8-13. This game controller is quite similar to the controllers you'll find on dedicated game consoles like the Microsoft Xbox and the Sony PS2, and it's suitable for most types of games. Unlike the other two controllers I've mentioned, this controller is also cordless, so you won't have to worry about ripping out the cord in the heat of an exciting game session.

Figure 8-13
A game pad is great for many different types of games.

Well, we've looked at a number of very nice extras for your home entertainment system PC in this chapter. I think you'll have to agree that the ideas and the interesting products I've shown you could really add a lot to the enjoyment of your home entertainment system PC. As I'm sure you can tell, my version of this project provides an awful lot of entertainment in a number of different areas.

Now that we've finished with the various hardware options, I'm going to dedicate the next chapter to showing you how to get the software functioning properly on your home entertainment system PC. If you've made it this far, you probably have a somewhat confusing collection of different applications sitting alongside your PC, but you may not know how to make everything work together. Well, never fear, because that's our topic next.

TESTING 1-2-3

At this point, you should have the following items completed:

❏ Your wireless keyboard and mouse are connected and functioning.

❏ If you are using a Pocket PC with your home entertainment system PC, you should have the software installed.

❏ Your game controllers should be ready to use.

Chapter 9

Software to Make It All Work

Tools of the Trade

To complete this chapter you will need the following:

The Drivers and Utilities CD-ROM that comes with the MSI motherboard

The ATI software CD-ROM that comes with the video board

The MSI DVD

Optional—Pinnacle Studio 8

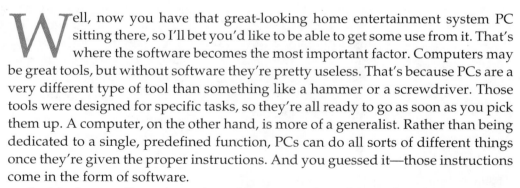

Well, now you have that great-looking home entertainment system PC sitting there, so I'll bet you'd like to be able to get some use from it. That's where the software becomes the most important factor. Computers may be great tools, but without software they're pretty useless. That's because PCs are a very different type of tool than something like a hammer or a screwdriver. Those tools were designed for specific tasks, so they're all ready to go as soon as you pick them up. A computer, on the other hand, is more of a generalist. Rather than being dedicated to a single, predefined function, PCs can do all sorts of different things once they're given the proper instructions. And you guessed it—those instructions come in the form of software.

In this chapter, I'm going to introduce you to the software that changes the PC you've just built into your home entertainment system PC. I'm not going to talk about ordinary software like spreadsheets and word processors because there are plenty of other books where you can find out about some of that stuff. Rather, I'm going to cover topics you won't find in a lot of other places. I'll tell you how to use the TV tuner application to pause live TV, for example. I'll make certain that you understand how to use the special settings on the home entertainment system PC to get the best possible sound. I'll even show you how you can make use of some simple video editing software to create your own DVD copies of content that you've saved on your home entertainment system PC. There will be some other interesting things along the way, so get ready to have some fun learning how to get the most entertainment possible from your home entertainment system PC.

Configuring the Audio Settings

I'd be willing to bet that you weren't too impressed with the first sounds that came from your home entertainment system PC. In all likelihood, the sound was flat and the surround sound effect didn't seem to be doing anything at all. You probably gave at least a bit of consideration to thinking that this whole fancy six-channel sound system was kind of a bust. To be honest, if you thought that, you were probably correct—at least the way the audio system was configured in the default setup, that is.

We're going to fix that now, and we'll start by installing the drivers.

TIPS OF THE TRADE

Why You Need to Adjust the Configuration

In case you're wondering why the default audio setup seems so lame, the answer is simple. A lot of people probably buy the same MSI motherboard that we've used for this project, slap it into a case, plug in a couple of those cheap PC speakers that sound like poor-quality tin cans, and never give a thought to how much they're missing. If the motherboard came configured for the setup we've used for the home entertainment system PC, anyone who didn't take advantage of the six-channel sound system would probably complain about how poor the sound quality was on MSI motherboards.

---

5 MINUTES

Installing the Audio Drivers

To install the proper audio drivers, first locate the Drivers and Utilities CD-ROM that came with the MSI motherboard. Then follow along with these steps:

1. Place the disc into the drive and wait while the Setup program launches.

2. Click the Avance AC97 Audio Drivers link.

3. Wait while the drivers are installed. When you see the message telling you that the setup is complete, as shown in Figure 9-1, click Finish to restart the home entertainment system PC and finalize the driver installation.

Figure 9-1
You must restart
the system to
finish the
installation.

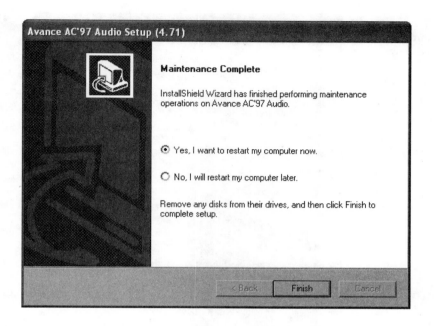

You can save yourself some time by installing the other drivers shown on the Setup screen before restarting the home entertainment system PC. At the very least, you'll want to install both the VIA Chipset Drivers and the VIA USB 2.0 Driver. The ADMtek Network Drivers do not have to be installed—Windows XP automatically installs the proper drivers for the network card as soon as the card is installed.

When you have finished installing all the drivers, make sure you remove the Drivers and Utilities disc and store it in a safe location. Personally, I like to keep all the discs and documentation for each system in separate small boxes that I clearly label with the system's name. Believe me, when you really need to install a driver or change a software installation, it's much easier (and far less stressful) if you can quickly find everything in one place.

Using the Audio Configuration Panel

Once the audio drivers are installed and you've restarted the system, you can configure the audio options. This is the step that will finally make your home entertainment system PC sound like it should sound. Once you've finished this step, you'll be amazed at the sounds from all six channels.

To open the audio configuration setup, follow these steps:

1. Click the Windows Start button to display the Start menu.

2. Click Control Panel (on the right side of the menu) to open the Control Panel, as shown in Figure 9-2. (If your Control Panel doesn't look like this, click the Switch To Classic View option in the task pane.)

Figure 9-2
The Control Panel
in classic view

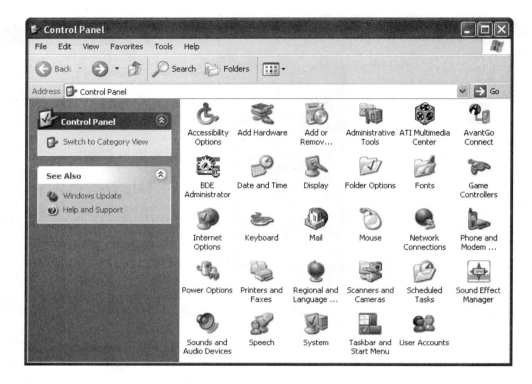

3. Double-click the Sound Effect Manager icon to open the AC97 Audio Configuration window, shown in Figure 9-3. You'll use this window to complete the audio configuration.

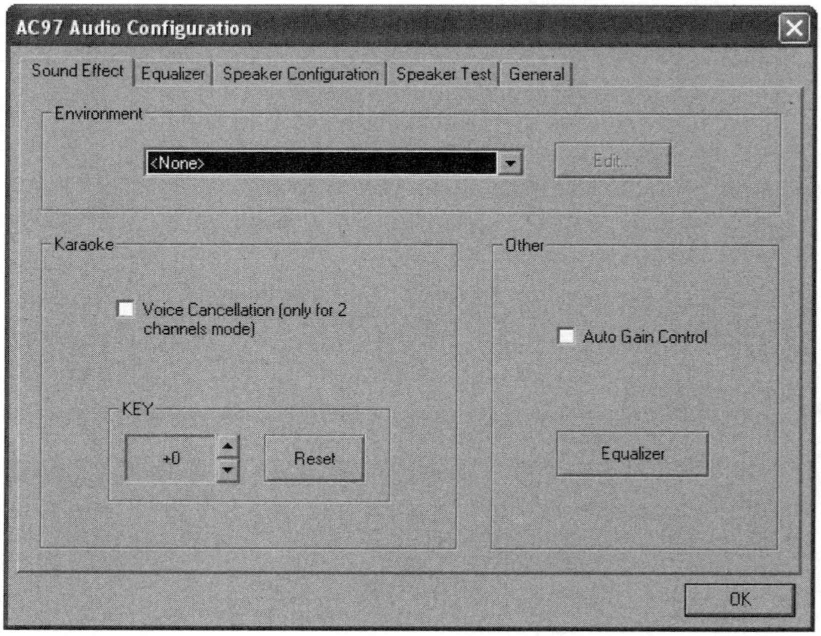

Figure 9-3
Use this window
to set up the audio
configuration options.

You can also open the AC97 Audio Configuration window by double-clicking the Sound Effect icon in the system tray—if it is visible there. The icon may be hidden, since Windows XP automatically hides unused system tray icons, so it's probably easier to simply use the Control Panel to open the window.

Setting the Sound Effects

The first tab you'll see when you open the AC97 Audio Configuration window is the Sound Effect tab, shown in Figure 9-3. Although these settings may be tempting to play with, it's generally best not to select anything on this tab. In fact, if the Environment setting is set to Generic (the default setting), I recommend that you select <None>. The reason for this is that the Environment setting changes the sound qualities by adding reverberation and by modifying the frequency response characteristics. When you select <None>, the sounds are not modified in this way, but rather are passed along to the speakers without added changes.

The settings in the Karaoke section are used to remove vocals from music. If Karaoke is your thing, feel free to experiment (but warn your neighbors so they can be away for the evening).

The Auto Gain Control option automatically adjusts the input level on the microphone input as sounds become loader or softer. If you intend to use voice recognition software, you should make sure that this option is not selected, since it will reduce the quality of the recognition.

Using the Sound Equalizer

Click the Equalizer tab (or the Equalizer button on the Sound Effect tab), shown in Figure 9-4. You can use the sliders on this tab to fine-tune the frequency response of the audio system.

Figure 9-4
These controls function as a graphic equalizer.

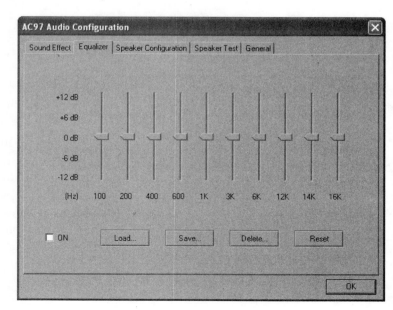

A graphic equalizer is more than a simple tone adjustment. I've found this type of control most useful when I'm recording old 78 RPM records onto audio CDs, because I'm able to boost the midrange frequencies while dropping off both the lowest and highest ones—thus cutting out low-frequency rumbles and high-frequency scratchiness. In fact, careful use of the graphic equalizer can greatly improve the sound in a number of similar situations.

5 MINUTES

Configuring the Speakers

Click the Speaker Configuration tab, shown in Figure 9-5. The initial default settings on this tab are the biggest cause of poor sound quality of any of the audio settings.

Figure 9-5
You must use the Speaker Configuration tab if you want more than two-channel sound.

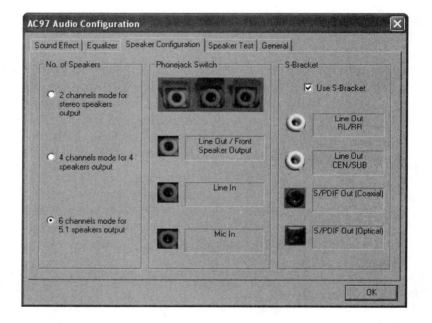

If you have a six-channel speaker system like the Altec Lansing system I've recommended for the home entertainment system PC, you'll want to select the 6 Channels Mode option. Otherwise, your rear speakers and your center channel speaker won't produce any sound. (If you have a four-channel speaker system, choose the 4 Channels Mode option.)

Notice that selecting either 4 Channels Mode or 6 Channels Mode modifies the functions of the line in and mic jacks on the I/O panel unless you also choose the Use S-Bracket option. In fact, if you choose either of these modes and do not have an S bracket, you will lose the use of the rear-panel line in jack (and the mic jack if you choose 6 Channels Mode). That's because those jacks must then serve the function of outputting sound to the rear and center channel speakers. As you can see, the Use S-Bracket option is very useful!

Next, click the Speaker Test tab, shown in Figure 9-6. You can click any of the speakers in the images to test the output. When you click a speaker icon, you should hear a sound from that speaker (and no other one). If some of the speakers don't work properly, you'll need to check the options on the Speaker Configuration tab again. If everything there seems to be correct, check all the speaker connections to make certain none of the plugs have been pulled out of their jacks. Notice that you can also swap the center channel and the subwoofer if necessary by selecting the Swap Center/Subwoofer Output option on the Speaker Test tab.

Figure 9-6
Test your speakers to make certain each of them is functioning properly.

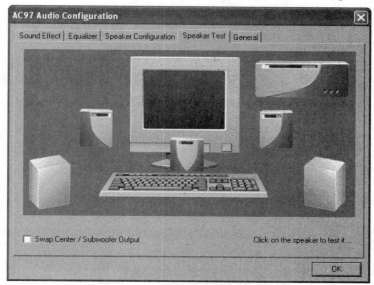

Click the General tab, shown in Figure 9-7. As you can tell, the settings on this tab aren't really very important to the audio configuration.

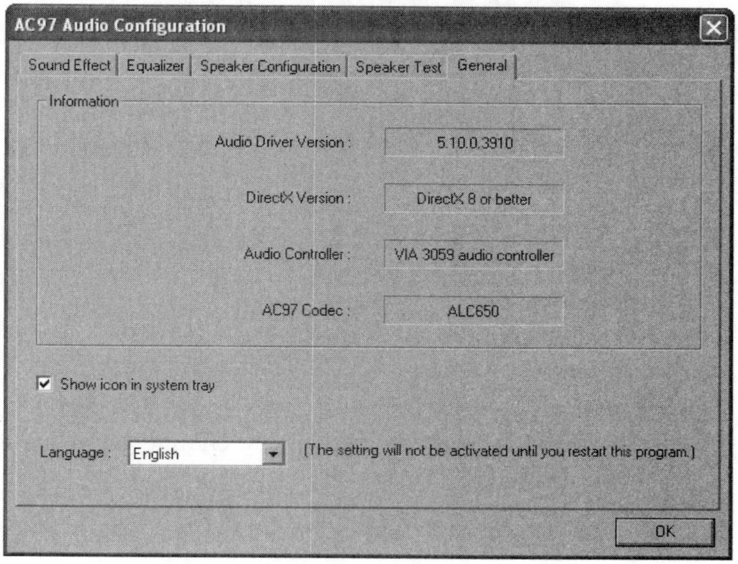

Figure 9-7
The General tab primarily provides driver version information.

Correcting Audio Stuttering

If you encounter a situation in which the TV application seems to produce almost a stuttering or echoing sound, you'll need to make an adjustment to one of the system BIOS settings to correct this problem. Otherwise, you'll find that the TV application may be almost unusable because the sound quality is so poor.

If you have this problem, here's what you need to do to correct it:

1. Restart your computer.

2. When the system is starting, press the DELETE key to enter the BIOS setup. (The key may be different if you have used a different motherboard.)

3. Use the arrow keys to navigate the opening menu of options in the BIOS setup utility and choose Advanced Chipset Features.

4. Press ENTER to display the options for this selection.

5. Move the highlight down to select AGP Timing Control.

6. Press ENTER to display the options for this selection.

7. Move the highlight down to the AGP Master 1 W/S Write option, as shown in Figure 9-8.

Figure 9-8
Select the AGP Master 1 W/S Write option.

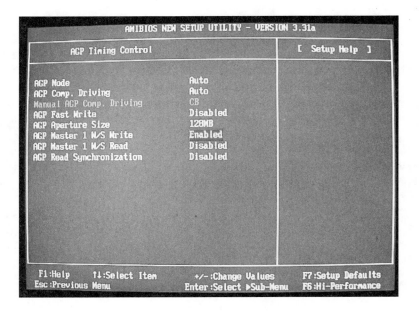

8. Press the plus key (+) to change the value to Enabled (the default is Disabled).

9. Press ESC twice to return to the main Setup screen.

10. Press F10 to save the changes and restart your computer.

Once you restart your home entertainment system PC, the audio stuttering problem should be gone. Isn't it amazing how such an obscure setting could affect the system's operation in such an odd manner?

Configuring the ATI Video Options

Next we'll turn to the video portion of your home entertainment system PC to make certain that it is set up for the best possible display. Some of this will be familiar if you've ever used a Windows-based PC before, but I'll try to concentrate on those areas that might otherwise be a bit confusing for you.

Installing the ATI Drivers

When you first turn on your home entertainment system PC after the video board is installed, Windows XP will locate and automatically install some semi-usable video drivers. Although these drivers will enable your video board to work, they don't provide full functionality, and they're certainly not the ones you'll want to use.

5 MINUTES

To install the proper drivers, you need to use the ATI software CD-ROM that comes with the video board. When you insert this disc, you'll see a window with a list of options. As you can probably guess without too much extra help, you want to click the Easy Install link to install the correct drivers.

I won't bore you with all the details of following along with the driver installation. You'll be able to simply follow the onscreen prompts to quickly complete the task. Once you have finished, come back here and we'll continue.

10 MINUTES ## Configuring the Video Display

Once you have the drivers installed, you'll want to properly configure the display. While most of the display property settings are simply cosmetic (and therefore, not something I'll discuss here), a few are very important. I'll touch on those important settings briefly.

To change the display properties, follow these steps:

1. Right-click a blank spot on the desktop and choose Properties from the pop-up menu to display the Display Properties dialog box.

2. Click the Settings tab, shown in Figure 9-9.

Figure 9-9
Use the Settings tab to adjust the resolution and number of colors.

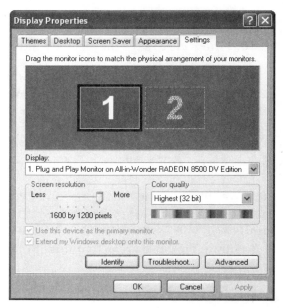

3. Drag the Screen Resolution slider to the right to select the screen resolution setting you prefer.

4. Make certain that the Color Quality selection is Highest (32 bit).

5. Click the Apply button and then confirm the new settings once the display has been readjusted.

6. Click the Advanced button to display the Advanced Settings dialog box.

7. Click the Monitor tab, shown in Figure 9-10.

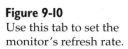

Figure 9-10
Use this tab to set the monitor's refresh rate.

8. Make certain that the Hide Modes That This Monitor Cannot Display option is selected.

9. Select the highest possible refresh rate from the Screen Refresh Rate drop-down list box. Note that in this case, I'm using the Planar LCD monitor, so a refresh rate of 60 Hz does not cause the flickering that it would on a standard CRT monitor. On a CRT monitor, you would want to select a rate of at least 70 Hz or more to prevent eye strain. In some cases, it might be necessary to choose a lower screen resolution in order to increase the refresh rate.

10. Click the Displays tab, shown in Figure 9-11.

Figure 9-11
Use this tab to enable or disable a display.

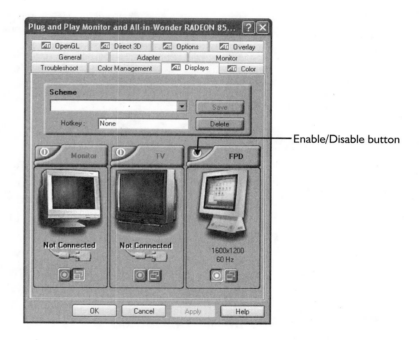

Enable/Disable button

11. To enable or disable the TV (or second monitor) display, click the Enable/ Disable button above the image of the display. You will want to disable the TV display when you are using the monitor so that you can enable the higher resolution/higher refresh rate mode.

12. Click OK to close the Advanced Settings dialog box.

13. Click OK to close the Display Properties dialog box.

There are a number of additional settings you may want to experiment with, but the ones I've discussed here are certainly some of the most important to your everyday enjoyment of the home entertainment system PC.

Configuring the ATI Multimedia Center

When you install the ATI drivers, you also install the ATI Multimedia Center, which is a group of applications that enable you to watch TV, play DVDs, play VCDs, play audio CDs, play various multimedia files stored on your home entertainment system PC, download free TV listings, and organize your multimedia content. You can access these applications using the Start menu or by using the ATI Multimedia Center LaunchPad—which appears along the right edge of the screen by default.

If you want to change the appearance of the LaunchPad, right-click it to display the pop-up menu shown in Figure 9-12 (I've also opened the Size submenu).

Figure 9-12
Use the pop-up menu to control the LaunchPad.

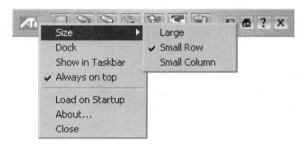

If you would rather use the Start menu and don't want your desktop cluttered with the LaunchPad icon, remove the check from the Load On Startup option. You can also drag the LaunchPad to a different location on the screen. For example, in Figure 9-12 I've dragged the LaunchPad away from the right edge of the screen so that it appears as a single row of small buttons.

By the way, you can easily identify any of the LaunchPad buttons by simply allowing the mouse pointer to hover over the button for a few seconds. When you do, a small ToolTip window will appear to show you the name of the button.

10 MINUTES

Setting the TV Options

The TV application, of course, enables you to watch TV shows on your home entertainment system PC. We'll have a closer look at using the TV application later in this chapter, but for now, let's take a look at the options for the ATI TV Player.

To set the TV options, follow these steps:

1. Open the ATI TV Player by selecting it from the Start menu (you will find it listed under ATI Multimedia Center in the All Programs menu) or by clicking the TV button on the LaunchPad (remember, you can hover your mouse over a button and the name will appear).

2. Click the Settings button (see Figure 9-13) to open the TV Player Setup dialog box.

Figure 9-13
Click Settings
to change the
TV options.

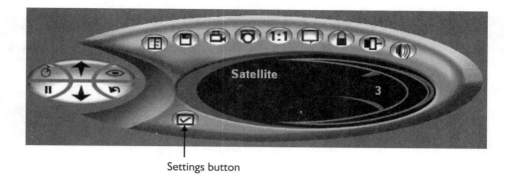

Settings button

3. On the TV Tuner tab, shown in Figure 9-14, you can edit the channel lineup by adding a check to the box for stations you want to be able to view, or remove the check for ones you don't want. For example, you might want to remove the check if a station's signal is so poor that you really can't watch the station. To change the name (or other properties) for the selected station, click the Details button. You can also select the type of input and you can click the Autoscan button to locate all TV signals.

Figure 9-14
Set the channel
options on the
TV Tuner tab.

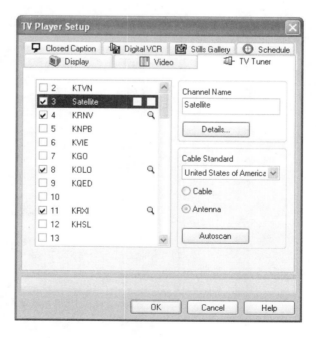

4. On the Video tab, shown in Figure 9-15, you can set the options that control the appearance of the TV picture. You can also choose which video input to use from the Connector drop-down list box (shown dropped down in the figure).

Figure 9-15
Use the Video tab to
adjust the appearance
of the TV image.

5. Use the Display tab, shown in Figure 9-16, to set the size of the TV
    image as well as to control some additional appearance options.

Figure 9-16
Choose the
display size on
the Display tab.

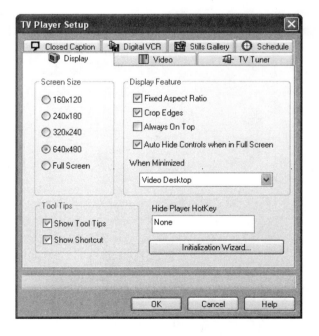

6. You can use the Closed Caption tab, shown in Figure 9-17, to enable
    the ATI TV Player to show closed captions, and to control how those
    captions are displayed. One very interesting feature you can enable on

this tab is the TV Magazine, which captures the closed captions to a text
file to produce a transcript of the shows you watch.

Figure 9-17
Use this tab to control
the closed caption
display.

7. Click the Digital VCR tab, shown in Figure 9-18, to set up the options
for recording TV shows on your hard drive. In addition to setting the
video quality and the amount of disk space to be used, you can click the
One Touch Record button to choose the settings for quick recordings at
the touch of a button. You can also see how much space is available for
recording videos.

Figure 9-18
Set your options for
recording TV shows
on your hard drive.

8. Move to the Stills Gallery tab, shown in Figure 9-19, to set the options for capturing still images from the ATI TV Player. This can be handy when you want to save a digital image or print a copy of whatever is appearing on the TV.

Figure 9-19
Use this tab to control still image captures.

9. Finally, you can use the Schedule tab, shown in Figure 9-20, to schedule events such as recording a transcript of your favorite TV news show. Click the Create New button to run the Schedule Wizard when you want to add a new scheduled event.

Figure 9-20
You can schedule events on this tab.

Although we breezed through the TV options fairly quickly, you now have a better idea about many of the options that are available to you. If you need a bit more information about specific settings, click the Help button to see the help screens for each of the options.

Setting the DVD Options

The ATI DVD Player settings are similar to the TV Player settings. For example, the Display tab of the DVD Setup dialog box, shown in Figure 9-21, is quite similar to the TV Setup dialog box Display tab previously shown in Figure 9-16.

Figure 9-21
The DVD Setup dialog box is quite similar to the TV Setup dialog box.

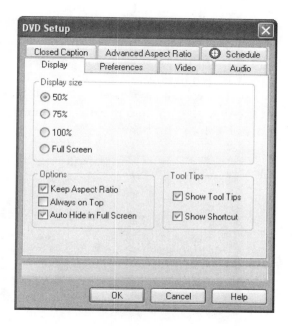

To be honest, though, you probably won't be using the ATI DVD Player to view DVD movies on your home entertainment system PC. The reason for this is quite simple—the MSI DVD Player software (which I'll cover a bit later in this chapter) has a number of advantages over the ATI DVD Player software. One very important advantage of the MSI DVD Player is its ability to make full use of the built-in six-channel sound capabilities on the MSI motherboard.

Setting the VCD, Audio CD, and File Player Options

As you have probably guessed by now, the ATI multimedia applications all share a lot of similar characteristics. Each of them looks very much alike, and each has similar controls. When you click the Settings button for any of them, you'll find quite similar settings options, too. Therefore, I'm not going to waste a lot of your time examining those options in detail. Besides, except for the TV Player, I think you'll probably find that some of the other programs on your home entertainment system PC—such as Windows Media Player and MusicMatch Jukebox—offer a better alternative to the somewhat limited capabilities of the ATI multimedia applications.

Installing the MSI DVD Player

To really take advantage of the sound capabilities of the onboard sound on the MSI motherboard, you'll want to install the MSI DVD Player. Although I haven't sampled every type of DVD player software you can buy, the MSI DVD Player is better than most, and it gives you access to the six-channel, Dolby 5.1 surround sound capabilities. In addition, the price is certainly right since the MSI DVD Player software is included with your MSI motherboard.

To install the MSI DVD Player, insert the MSI DVD disc and wait for the screen shown in Figure 9-22 to appear. Then, click the Install Software link and follow the onscreen instructions. You will need the serial number that is printed on the disc to complete the installation, so you may want to write down that number before you begin.

Figure 9-22
Install the MSI DVD Player to take advantage of the motherboard's sound capabilities.

Using the MSI DVD Player

Figure 9-23 shows the MSI DVD Player. I've added callouts to help you identify the major controls. In most cases, you should have little trouble using the MSI DVD Player since the controls it uses are pretty much the same as those you would find on any DVD player.

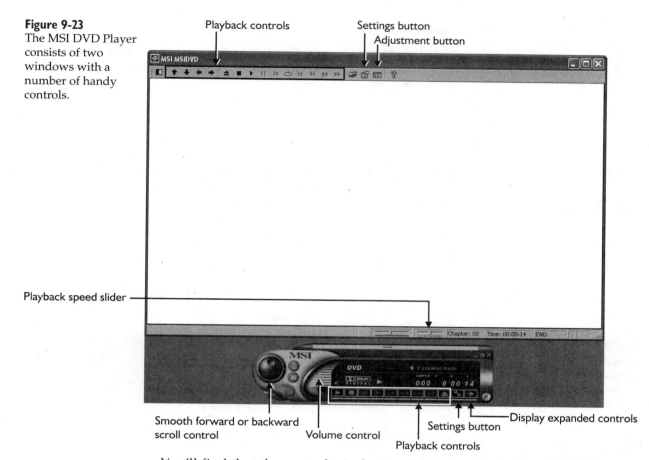

Figure 9-23
The MSI DVD Player consists of two windows with a number of handy controls.

Playback controls

Settings button

Adjustment button

Playback speed slider

Smooth forward or backward scroll control

Volume control

Playback controls

Settings button

Display expanded controls

You'll find that the control window and the viewer window share many of the same controls, so you can use whichever set you prefer. In addition, the ATI Remote Control can also be used to control the MSI DVD Player. You don't have to do anything special to use the ATI Remote Control with the MSI DVD Player, either. When the MSI DVD Player is running, the ATI Remote Control automatically sends its commands to the MSI DVD Player. This is just another example of just how well integrated the various components of your home entertainment system PC actually are.

10 MINUTES

Configuring the MSI DVD Player

The MSI DVD Player has several options that you can use to control various aspects of DVD, VCD, and audio CD playback. You may, however, find that setting these options seems a little confusing since certain options can only be adjusted while a disc is actually in the drive. This is not, however, something that is unique to the MSI DVD Player—every DVD player I've ever encountered works the same way. The reason for this is simple, though. Certain settings really are specific to the capabilities included on the disc that you are playing. Let's take a quick look at the various settings options.

Setting the General Properties

When you click the Settings button, the first thing you will see is the General tab of the Properties dialog box, shown in Figure 9-24. Here you can select a number of options that control the view of the MSI DVD Player window. For example, you can remove the toolbar or the status bar from the DVD Player window, or you can remove the separate player control window by using the options in the View area.

Figure 9-24
This tab controls the MSI DVD Player window components.

HEADS **UP!**

Don't Touch the Region Setting!

Unfortunately, the General tab has a very dangerous option that could cause you all sorts of grief. By agreement of the manufacturers of DVD players, all DVD players worldwide recognize the region coding that is contained on many DVD movie discs. For some reason, this agreement attempts to limit your ability to view DVDs from other regions by limiting to a total of five the number of times a DVD player can be switched to a different region. That is, if you either watch a DVD that has region coding for another region or manually switch your DVD player to another region, you'll reduce the number of times you can switch regions by one. To make matters worse, the fifth region that is viewed becomes permanent, and the DVD player can no longer be switched to a different region. So, for example, if you happen to select region 2 and click the Apply button, you'll only have three remaining region switches left. If you then switch back to region 1, you'll be down to two. As you can tell, you could easily render your DVD player incapable of playing locally available DVDs. Fortunately, this section of the tab is not available when a DVD is playing—I wish you could disable it completely (since there's no real reason to manually switch regions, because playing a DVD from another region automatically makes the switch).

Setting Up the Audio Properties

Next we'll take a look at the Audio tab, shown in Figure 9-25. This tab has some very important settings that enable you to get the full benefit from your home entertainment system PC's six-channel audio system.

Figure 9-25
Use this tab to enable six-channel audio.

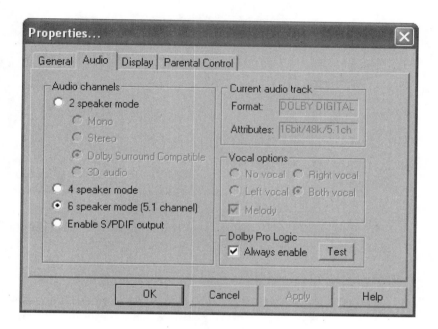

By default, the 2 Speaker Mode option is selected. To get the full surround sound effect, you'll want to choose 6 Speaker Mode (5.1 Channel) whenever the option is available (it will only be available when a DVD movie that supports Dolby 5.1 surround sound is being played). Or, you may want to select the Enable S/PDIF Output option if you're using a digital audio connection to your component receiver.

Choosing the Display Properties

Next we'll move to the Display tab, shown in Figure 9-26. Since the home entertainment system PC has plenty of computing power, you will see the best image by selecting all the check boxes under Custom Quality Options (which will happen automatically if you select the High radio button under Quality).

Figure 9-26
These controls affect
the video quality.

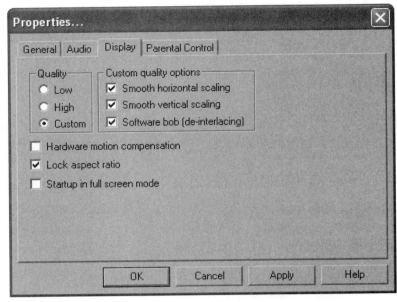

You may also want to select all three of the options in the lower section of this
tab. Once again, these are options that will optimize the display of DVD movies,
and your home entertainment system PC has plenty of power to handle them.

Using the Parental Controls

The Parental Control tab, shown in Figure 9-27, enables you to decide the highest
acceptable movie ratings that can be displayed. If you set this option, no one will
be able to play movies above your set limit. You can also set a password to
prevent anyone from setting a higher rating level.

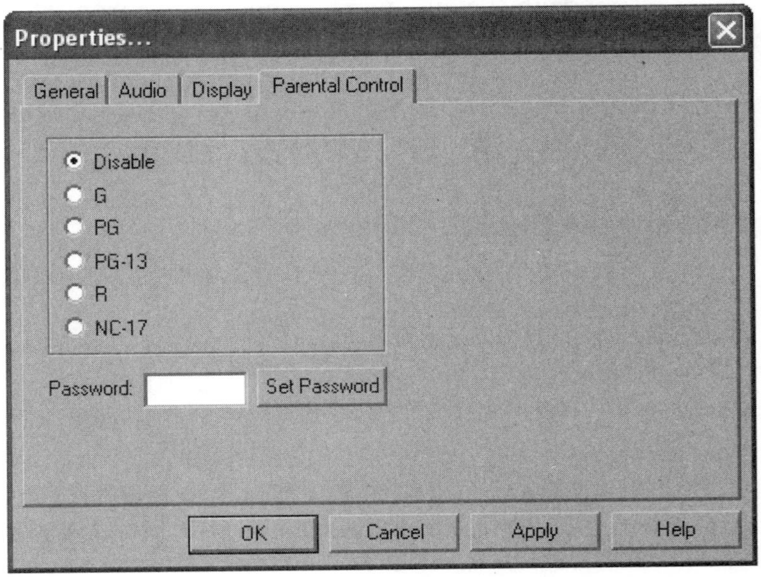

Figure 9-27
Parental Controls put
the burden of limiting
unacceptable movies
where it belongs—on
the parent.

Adjusting the Audio and Video

The final MSI DVD Player settings we'll look at are the adjustments shown in Figure 9-28. These controls appear when you click the Adjustment button (refer to Figure 9-23), and they enable you to change the volume, the brightness, and the color mix. You'll find these adjustments particularly useful for making certain DVD movies easier to see—especially those that were filmed quite dark.

Figure 9-28
These controls can make DVD movies more visible.

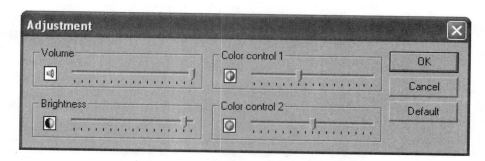

Using the TV Application

The TV application is really at the heart of the home entertainment system PC project, and yet it's probably the one part of the whole project that you'll find the most confusing at first. Oh, you'll probably be able to do ordinary television watching with no trouble at all, but I have no doubt that some of the more advanced features will seem just as clear as mud in the beginning. Well, don't let that bother you, because I've waded through the program and will show you how to make this amazing application do its thing. I'm sure you'll be very pleasantly surprised at just how much better your TV watching experience will become once you know how to put the home entertainment system PC to the task.

Understanding the TV Modes

The ATI TV Player has two different modes of operation. The normal mode is the one in which you simply watch TV the way you would with a regular TV set. In this mode, you can schedule recordings using the digital VCR function pretty much the same way that you would schedule a recording with your existing VCR (except that you won't have to deal with a display that is constantly blinking 12:00).

In addition to the normal mode, the ATI TV Player offers *TV-On-Demand* mode. In this mode, you can pause live TV, watch an instant replay of something you just saw, skip the commercials, and just generally make watching TV a whole lot more convenient. Essentially, TV-On-Demand mode enables your home entertainment system PC to act like a TiVo or ReplayTV, except with many more capabilities.

Something You Need to Know About Video Modes

There is one very important thing to remember about the two video modes—you cannot use the digital VCR to schedule a recording while you are using TV-On-Demand mode. The reason for this is simple. During TV-On-Demand mode operation, your home entertainment system PC is constantly recording the incoming video into a file, which enables you to move forward and backward through the video.

You can, however, export the delayed video that was recorded during TV-On-Demand mode. The exported file can then be edited in a video editing program (I'll discuss this later in the chapter), saved for later viewing, or even shared with another PC.

The TV controller changes slightly to indicate which mode is currently active. Figure 9-29 shows how the controller appears during normal mode.

Figure 9-29
The TV Player is running in normal mode.

Click this button to switch between modes

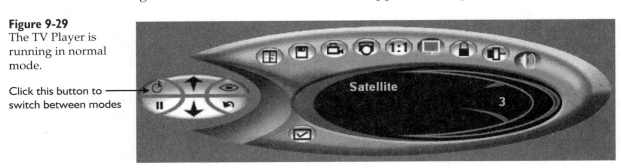

Figure 9-30 shows how the TV appears when TV-On-Demand mode is active.

Figure 9-30
Now the TV Player is in TV-On-Demand mode.

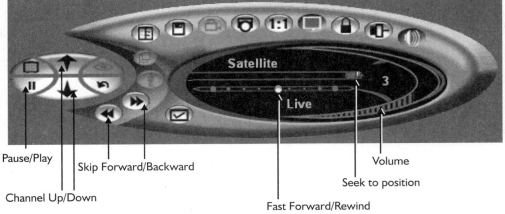

Pause/Play

Channel Up/Down

Skip Forward/Backward

Fast Forward/Rewind

Seek to position

Volume

Using TV-On-Demand

TV-On-Demand mode enables you to treat live TV pretty much like a recording that you made earlier. That is, you might want to think of TV-On-Demand mode as the equivalent of watching TV shows that you recorded on your VCR at some earlier time—but with the important difference being that TV-On-Demand mode continues to record the live broadcast even when you pause, fast forward, or rewind. To make this a little clearer, consider the following scenario:

❏ Your local news broadcast starts each evening at 5:00 P.M.—the same time that you leave the office heading home.

❏ You like to prepare dinner and eat as soon as you get home, and this typically takes until about 6:30.

❏ At 6:30 you sit down to watch TV, but then your sister calls and talks for 15 minutes about the plans for another relative's upcoming birthday party.

❏ At 6:45 you finally start watching the 5:00 P.M. news broadcast that your home entertainment system PC started recording in TV-On-Demand mode.

❏ Since you don't want to watch all the commercials, you can watch a typical hour of broadcast TV in about 38 minutes. You also decide to skip the sports segment, saving another ten minutes.

❏ By 9:45 P.M. you will have caught up to the live broadcast that started at 5:00 P.M., but instead of sitting in front of the TV for almost five hours, you'll have been there for three hours.

Okay, so maybe you don't want to watch that much TV every night, but just think about how much more you'll be able to do if you can watch the same TV shows in three hours instead of five hours. If you saved two hours a day, five days a week, the time would add up to over 500 hours a year. If you have a 40-hour-a-week job, that's like getting over 12 weeks of extra vacation time every year!

Now that you have a better understanding of the TV-On-Demand mode, using it should be simple. Figure 9-30 identified all the important controls you'll use (remember that you can also use the ATI remote control). Don't forget that you must start the TV Player in TV-On-Demand mode so that it can record the live TV broadcast you'll view later. I'll show you how to do this automatically in the next section.

Scheduling TV Player Events

It's pretty clear that you'll want the TV Player to automatically start capturing live video well ahead of when you might want to begin watching TV. That way, you'll be able to rewind the broadcast so that you can view your favorite TV shows minus all of those commercial breaks, and on your own schedule. To do this, you can simply schedule an event.

Here's what you need to do to schedule a TV Player event:

1. With the TV Player open, click the Settings button (refer back to Figure 9-13) and then click the Schedule tab.

2. On the Schedule tab of the TV Player Setup dialog box (refer back to Figure 9-20), click the Create New button to start the Schedule Wizard.

3. Click Next to continue.

4. Select Watch A TV Program from the drop-down list.

5. Click Next to continue.

6. Enter a name for the event and choose how often to run it, as shown in Figure 9-31.

Figure 9-31
Name and choose the frequency of the event.

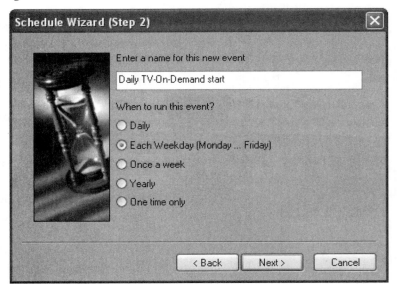

7. Click Next to continue.

8. Set the start time.

9. Click Next to continue.

10. Select the Yes, I Want To Set It Up (If Available) option, as shown in Figure 9-32. This will enable you to make certain that the TV Player automatically records the correct channel even if you've been watching a different one.

Figure 9-32
Make certain you
choose to set up the
recording settings.

11. Click Next to continue.

12. Make certain that Analog TV Tuner is selected. This will ensure that you record from the TV tuner card.

13. Click Next to continue.

14. Choose the channel you want to watch.

15. Click Next to continue.

16. Verify that the correct settings are shown (see Figure 9-33) and click the Finish button to add the event to the schedule.

Figure 9-33
Click Finish to
compete the
scheduling.

If you want to have the TV tuner automatically change the channels during the TV-On-Demand recording, just set up another event that specifies the correct time and channel. You can set up as many different channel changes as you like.

Be sure to leave the TV Player in TV-On-Demand mode so that your scheduled events are available for viewing when you want to watch them. Then sit back and enjoy TV on your own schedule!

Using the Guide Plus+ TV Listings

The ATI TV Player has yet another trick for making your TV viewing more convenient. This is the Guide Plus+ TV program guide shown in Figure 9-34.

Figure 9-34
You can use Guide Plus+ to schedule your TV viewing and recordings.

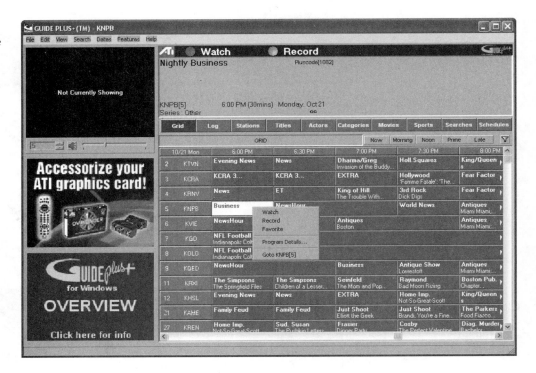

Using the Guide Plus+ system, you can view the TV listings in a number of different ways. You have the option of viewing a schedule grid, as shown in Figure 9-34, or choosing a different view, such as all the shows for one station, shows by title, and so on. If you want to record one of the shows, just right-click it and choose Record from the pop-up menu.

Guide Plus+ downloads the TV listings from the Internet. You are required to provide a minimal amount of information to register, but the listings themselves are free (okay, so you do have to put up with a small ad pane along the left side of the Guide Plus+ window, but that's pretty easy to ignore).

Recordings that you schedule using the Guide Plus+ system automatically appear in your TV Player's schedule. This means that you can easily go through the program listings, adding the specific programs you want to watch (or record). The whole process couldn't be any simpler or more enjoyable.

Recording Directly to DVD

As I'm writing this, InterVideo has just announced a new product called WinDVD Recorder. Although I wasn't able to check it out in time to cover it for the book, WinDVD Recorder is supposed to function very much like the TV-On-Demand feature of the ATI TV application, but with an important difference. In addition to allowing you to record your favorite TV shows to your hard drive, WinDVD Recorder can also record directly to DVD.

To find out more about WinDVD Recorder, visit the InterVideo web site at www.intervideo.com.

Using Windows Media Player

If you have used a PC at all in the past few years, you've no doubt encountered the Windows Media Player. What you might not realize, however, is how the Windows Media Player might be useful on your home entertainment system PC. In this section, I'll concentrate on showing you how to make use of some features of the Windows Media Player that will be of particular interest on your home entertainment system PC.

Ripping Content with the Windows Media Player

One of the more useful features of your home entertainment system PC is its ability to store and then deliver various types of multimedia content on demand. A good example of this is the way that you can store the equivalent of hundreds of audio CDs on the home entertainment system PC's hard drive, and then play that music in whatever combination of tracks you want without ever touching the audio CDs again. It turns out that Windows Media Player is an excellent (and free) tool for this job.

By the way, the term for copying audio CD contents to your hard drive is *ripping*. Because your home entertainment system PC is equipped with a high-quality CD drive, ripping is done digitally rather than as an analog process, so an entire audio CD can be ripped to your hard drive in just a few minutes.

When you place an audio CD into the drive, Windows Media Player uses your Internet connection to attempt to locate the album details. This is an awfully handy feature, because as Figure 9-35 shows, there is a lot of information available about most audio CDs.

Figure 9-35
Windows Media
Player automatically
downloads the details
on your audio CDs.

To copy an audio CD to your hard drive, follow these steps:

1. Insert the audio CD in the drive. (Windows Media Player should start automatically unless you've installed another program that has associated itself with audio CDs—if Windows Media Player does not start, select it from the Windows Start menu.)

2. Click the Copy From CD button on the Windows Media Player taskbar. (If the Windows Media Player taskbar is hidden, you may first have to return to full mode by pressing CTRL-1.)

3. Click the Copy Music button to begin ripping the music tracks to your hard drive.

4. When all the tracks have been copied, click the Media Library button in the Windows Media Player taskbar to view the music you have copied (see Figure 9-36).

Figure 9-36
Music you have copied appears in the Media Library.

Creating Playlists

Once you have copied music to your hard drive, you can use the New Playlist button to create as many different groups of songs as you like. You can then use the Add To Playlist button to add selected cuts to the playlist. Essentially, you'll be creating your own mixes, so you can program music for parties, quiet listening, or whatever you prefer.

Playlists become especially important when you want to create—*burn*—your own audio CDs using tracks from different audio CDs that you've ripped. In order to be playable in most audio CD players, you must burn all the tracks in a single session. By creating a playlist containing all the tracks you want to include, you ensure that the tracks are all added at once. In Figure 9-37, I've created a playlist that includes songs from two different albums by the Austin Lounge Lizards—one of my favorites.

Figure 9-37
Create playlists of
your favorite music.

By the way, you can drag and drop tracks in the playlist if you want to change
the order in which they are played. There are also up and down arrow buttons on
the Windows Media Player toolbar that you can use for this purpose, but I find
the drag-and-drop method easier to use.

Recording Audio CDs with the Windows Media Player

You can also use the Windows Media Player to create audio CDs from the music
that you've ripped. This might come in handy if you want to create audio CDs to
play in your car, because you can fill the entire length of the CD with your
favorite music (rather than putting up with audio CDs that won't last through
your drive).

To create your own audio CDs, follow these steps:

1. Place a blank CD-R disc into the drive.

2. Click the Copy To CD Or Device button on the Windows Media
    Player taskbar.

3. Select the playlist or album you want to copy, as shown in
    Figure 9-38.

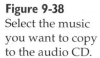

Figure 9-38
Select the music
you want to copy
to the audio CD.

4. If any of the tracks are listed as "Will not fit," you'll need to remove some tracks from the copy by deselecting them. In this case, I have 76 minutes' worth of tracks selected, and they'll fit easily onto the 80-minute CD-R disc.

5. Click the Copy Music button to begin copying the tracks.

As an alternative to using Windows Media Player, you may want to consider MusicMatch Jukebox. Some PC users prefer it to Windows Media Player, but I personally feel that Windows Media Player works just as well. Not only that, but MusicMatch Jukebox limits the recording speed for audio CDs to 1X unless you buy an upgrade. The Windows Media Player will burn discs at the maximum speed allowed by your drive.

Creating DVD Movies

I'm only going to touch briefly on this final subject because it's really not possible to do justice to the subject of creating DVD movies in a few pages. Rather, I'm just going to point out that the configuration of your home entertainment system PC is perfect for video editing and creating your own DVD movies. I am, however, going to show you a glimpse of a very nice piece of software I've found to be perfect for this task.

If you have a digital camcorder, you probably have some "free" video editing software that came bundled with the camcorder. You may also have some video editing software that came bundled with your DVD-R/RW drive. In either case, if you've tried using that software, you may have come to the same conclusion that I have—none of that "OEM" software is really worth very much. That's why I'm going to recommend something a little better—Pinnacle Studio 8 (see Figure 9-39).

One of the reasons I like Pinnacle Studio 8 is that, to me, this software is a major improvement over those bundled video editing packages, while at the

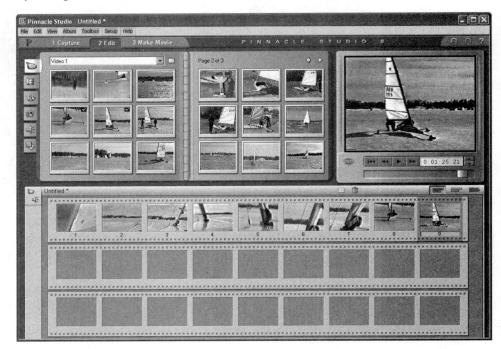

Figure 9-39
Pinnacle Studio 8 is a big step up from OEM video editing software.

same time it is far less expensive and easier to use than something like Adobe Premiere. With Pinnacle Studio 8, you have your choice of storyboard, timeline, or text views, so you are in charge. I don't care for video editing software that tries to make all the decisions, because that makes it hard for you to really be in charge of your movie. You can find out more about Pinnacle Studio 8 on the Web at www.pinnaclesys.com.

The Conclusion

Well, there you have it. If you've been following along and building your home entertainment system PC, you now have the most useful, fun, and versatile pieces of home entertainment equipment you could find anywhere. I've used this chapter to wrap up the project by showing you how to bring it all together with the proper software. Now it's time for you to go and play some. After all, you built your home entertainment system PC for enjoyment, and now you're ready to reap the rewards. Enjoy!

At this point, you should have completed the following items:

❑ Installed the audio drivers and configured your audio options

❑ Installed the video drivers and configured your display

❑ Set up your TV tuner and DVD playback options

❑ Mastered how to record your favorite TV shows

A Shopping List

Building the home entertainment system PC is an interesting project, but you really need to buy all the necessary components before you start building if you want the whole process to go as smoothly as possible. So to make things a little easier for you, I've assembled a shopping list that contains everything you'll need. That way, you won't have to make up your list by going through each chapter on your own.

I've also listed some web sites at which you can buy many of the home entertainment system PC components. These aren't, of course, the only places where you can buy what you need, but they are some places I've found to be reliable. Remember, though, that a good local PC store may offer a bit more help if you run into anything you don't quite understand.

The Basics

Here's the list of basic components you'll want to buy to get your home entertainment system PC project off the ground. Remember that manufacturers often replace products with newer, upgraded models, so if you don't find the exact item I've listed, check for a newer version that does the job.

❏ Antec Plus660AMG case (www.antec-inc.com)

❏ MSI KT3 Ultra2-R motherboard (www.msi.com)

❏ AMD Athlon XP 2200+ processor (www.amd.com)

❑ TaiSol ball-bearing fan–equipped heat sink for AMD Athlon XP processors (buy this with the CPU)

❑ Crucial Technology memory—two 512MB PC2700 DDR memory modules (www.crucial.com)

❏ ATI All-In-Wonder Radeon 8500DV video board with TV tuner (www.ati.com)

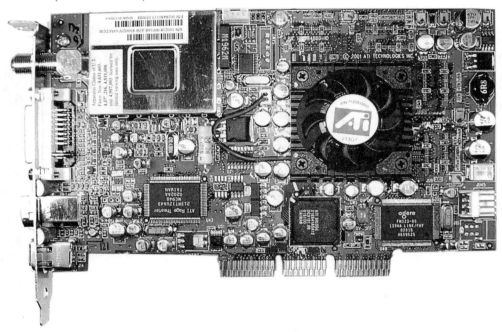

❏ Maxtor D540X 160GB Ultra ATA/133 hard drive (www.maxtor.com)

❏ Generic 3.5-inch disk drive (no need to be picky about a brand)

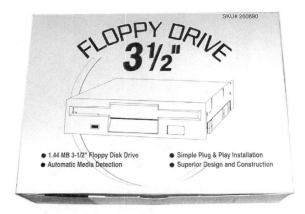

❏ Pioneer DVR-104 DVD-R/RW drive (www.pioneerelectronics.com)

❏ Altec Lansing model 5100 speaker system (www.alteclansing.com)

❑ Planar PL201M-BK LCD monitor (www.planar.com)

❑ Logitech Cordless Freedom Optical keyboard (www.logitech.com)

❑ Windows XP Professional or Windows XP Home Edition
(www.microsoft.com)

Optional Add-Ons

In addition to the basics, you may want to consider the following optional components. None of these is absolutely essential, but each of them will really enhance your home entertainment system PC.

❑ Terk TV5 amplified indoor TV antenna (www.terk.com)

❑ Terk Leapfrog WaveMaster 20 home broadcast system (www.terk.com)

❑ MSI S bracket for the MSI KT3 Ultra2 series motherboard (www.msi.com)

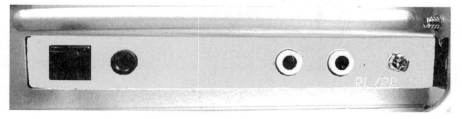

❑ MSI Bluetooth kit for the MSI KT3 Ultra2-R series motherboard (www.msi.com)

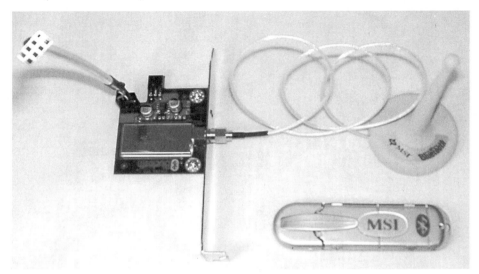

❑ Proxim WiFi Access Point (www.proxim.com)

❑ Linksys Ethernet adapter (www.linksys.com)

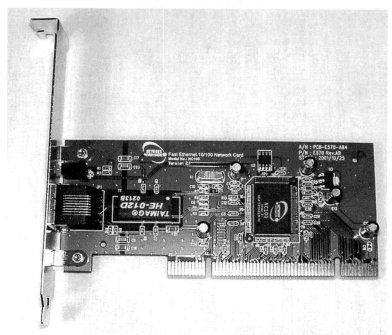

❑ Copernic Agent Professional (www.copernic.com)

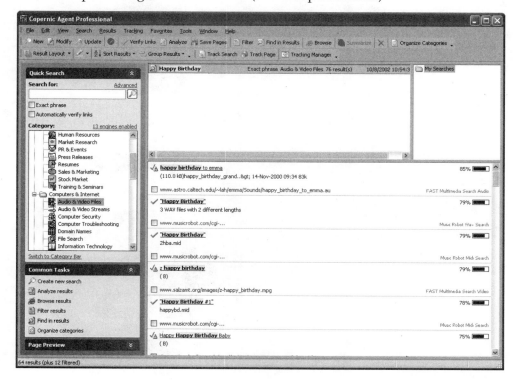

❏ Logitech Cordless Optical TrackMan trackball (www.logitech.com)

❏ Logitech WingMan Extreme Digital 3D joystick (www.logitech.com)

❏ Logitech WingMan Formula Force GP racing wheel (www.logitech.com)

❑ Logitech WingMan Cordless Rumblepad game pad (www.logitech.com)

❑ UPS (not brand specific—buy at least a 350 VA unit from your local computer or office supply store)

Online Sources

If you aren't lucky enough to have a discount computer superstore in your neighborhood, you'll probably find yourself shopping for the home entertainment system PC components online. If so, it's nice to have an idea where to begin. Here are some of the online merchants I've dealt with successfully:

❑ PC Nation (www.pcnation.com)

❑ Chumbo.com (www.chumbo.com)

❑ Jazz Technology Computer Superstore (jazz.zoovy.com)

❑ Googlegear (www.googlegear.com)

When you're shopping for the home entertainment system PC components online, remember to check to make sure the components you order are in stock. Also, be sure to check on the shipping and handling—some of these merchants offer free shipping from time to time for orders above a specified value.

Index

References to figures and illustrations are in italics.

INTERNATIONAL CONTACT INFORMATION

AUSTRALIA
McGraw-Hill Book Company Australia Pty. Ltd.
TEL +61-2-9900-1800
FAX +61-2-9878-8881
http://www.mcgraw-hill.com.au
books-it_sydney@mcgraw-hill.com

CANADA
McGraw-Hill Ryerson Ltd.
TEL +905-430-5000
FAX +905-430-5020
http://www.mcgraw-hill.ca

GREECE, MIDDLE EAST, & AFRICA
(Excluding South Africa)
McGraw-Hill Hellas
TEL +30-210-6560-990
TEL +30-210-6560-993
TEL +30-210-6560-994
FAX +30-210-6545-525

MEXICO (Also serving Latin America)
McGraw-Hill Interamericana Editores S.A. de C.V.
TEL +525-117-1583
FAX +525-117-1589
http://www.mcgraw-hill.com.mx
fernando_castellanos@mcgraw-hill.com

SINGAPORE (Serving Asia)
McGraw-Hill Book Company
TEL +65-863-1580
FAX +65-862-3354
http://www.mcgraw-hill.com.sg
mghasia@mcgraw-hill.com

SOUTH AFRICA
McGraw-Hill South Africa
TEL +27-11-622-7512
FAX +27-11-622-9045
robyn_swanepoel@mcgraw-hill.com

SPAIN
McGraw-Hill/Interamericana de España, S.A.U.
TEL +34-91-180-3000
FAX +34-91-372-8513
http://www.mcgraw-hill.es
professional@mcgraw-hill.es

UNITED KINGDOM, NORTHERN,
EASTERN, & CENTRAL EUROPE
McGraw-Hill Education Europe
TEL +44-1-628-502500
FAX +44-1-628-770224
http://www.mcgraw-hill.co.uk
computing_neurope@mcgraw-hill.com

ALL OTHER INQUIRIES Contact:
Osborne/McGraw-Hill
TEL +1-510-549-6600
FAX +1-510-883-7600
http://www.osborne.com
omg_international@mcgraw-hill.com

YOUR WAY OR **THE HIGHWAY.**

We Know What You Want.

You demand a computing experience that fits your needs. We understand. That's why Antec's products are as demanding as you. So here's the new PlusView – with all the features of our award-winning Performance Plus cases, our high-clarity side window, and without a power supply. Pick from Antec's high performance power, cooling, and illumination products to customize a PC that's done only one way – yours. That's *the Power of You*.
To view our full line of products, visit us at www.antec-inc.com

Antec
The Power of You

Upgrade Solutions

If you're looking for low prices on top-quality RAM, look no further than Crucial Technology.

As a division of Micron, one of the world's largest memory chip manufacturers, Crucial offers low prices on the highest quality RAM on the market. Whether you're shopping for memory for a specific system or just want to see a list of parts, our Web site always has up-to-the-minute pricing information.

Your direct source for the highest-quality, most compatible memory upgrades available, with over 94,000 upgrades for more than 15,000 systems.

Order memory from crucial.com and get:

- **Convenient, secure online ordering**
- **Competitive pricing**
- **10% online discount**
- **Guaranteed compatibility or your money back**
- **Unparalleled customer service and free technical support**
- **Limited lifetime warranty**

crucial ™

TECHNOLOGY

A Division of Micron

Save money and do it yourself !

These highly visual, step-by-step, show-and-tell guides provide you with hands-on success!

■ **Build Your Own PC Home Entertainment System**
by Brian Underdahl • 0-07-222769-9

■ **Build Your Own High Performance Gamers' Mod PC**
by Joel Durham & Edward Chen • 0-07-222901-2

■ **Build Your Own PC Recording Studio**
by Jon Chappell • 0-07-222904-7

■ **Build Your Own Server**
by Tony Caputo • 0-07-222728-1

OSBORNE
www.osborne.com